Uncommon Love

Uncommon
LOVE

How to Survive
a Love Affair

L.M. Edelhaus

Prism Publishing & Seminars

PRISM PUBLISHING & SEMINARS
P.O. BOX 153
SAUGERTIES, NY 12477

Printed in the United States by Thomson-Shore

Library of Congress Catalogue Card Number: 96-70517
ISBN 0-9653286-0-0: $12.95

10 9 8 7 6 5 4 3 2 1

For My Dear Friend

Introduction

Why do we have love affairs? It is because there is nothing like passionate love, nothing; most of us want it in our lives, and we want it very much. We are very fortunate when we can experience it once in our lives. We are very, *very* fortunate when we are allowed to have passionate love in a legitimate context – in a lifelong, open, daily connection with our loved one which will enrich the tapestry of our lives and fulfill our deep longing for the Other Self. This book is written for people who are involved in, or thinking about being involved in, another kind of passionate love: an extra-marital love relationship – a love affair. The partners in a love affair face unique difficulties and especially confusing ambiguities; at the same time, they have embarked upon what certainly is one of the richest, most generative and enlightening of human experiences.

There is an ideal that the word "passion" reflects. It indicates our ability and desire to let ourselves "be carried" into one of the most significant experiences of our lives, to be able safely to let go of control and relax into love. But in a love affair, we cannot "relax into love." Passionate love comes our way, but there is an obstacle on the path to enrichment and fulfillment, and this obstacle is the marriage of one or both of the parties – marriage not just to another person, but to a whole life that may include children, relatives, property, community, and a system of established and comfortable rhythms embedded in the day, the week, the season, the year.

It is risky to speak seriously about love affairs while speaking of marriage as an "obstacle." One might feel one's hackles rising, a slight irritation; what about the deep affection and caring that comes with a long marriage, with a lifetime spent together on births and deaths, struggles with money, raising children, illnesses, joys and sorrows? Surely this is a better love: more stable, deep, and "real." Why should we even discuss this other, "illicit" love in the same breath?

The problem is that unless the love in marriage is sufficiently fulfilling and generative for both parties, it is vulnerable – either to a passion that materializes in the form of another person, or perhaps only to our own imagination, our longing, our sense that something is "missing." We may shrug these feelings off, reason that we can't have everything, and that after 15 (20, 25, 30) years, passion is too much to ask, and compared to the strong ties that bind us, frivolous. Who needs it? We have everything we could reasonably have expected from our lives and we should count our blessings. But if this is the truth of the matter, how can we explain our eternal interest in the subject of passionate love, temptation in marriage, what it is really like to have a love affair, and so on? One has only to think about movies, television talk shows, news stories about celebrities and famous personalities, daytime soaps, and romance novels, not to mention a great deal of classic literature. The subject is of widespread interest and fascination for almost everyone, regardless of social position or intellectual level. The **Readers' Guide to Periodical Literature** reflects our interest very well; it actually has a heading for "Love Affairs" (under which it says, "See 'Adultery'." "Adultery" has several entries per edition.).

"Passion" is not misnamed. The Latin origin of the word is "pati" or "patior," which means *to suffer, to experience, to submit to*. The same root is the basis of the word "passive," and also of the word "patient," both in the sense of *enduring quietly* and of *receiving care for an illness*.

We often feel helpless, "passive," in the face of passion, powerless to prevent ourselves from being swept away. Typically, neither religion, morality, duty, nor reason is enough to stop our going forth to meet the promise of this incredible sweetness, this anticipation of astonishing joy. Nothing is enough to stop passion from having its way with us. If the path is free and clear, then we are free to drink of the cup and to be confident that it will constantly be refilled. But in the other circumstance, where there is an already-existing commitment, we will also experience the other side of the coin – consternation, bittersweet disappointment, and shocking sharp pain. This is the subject matter of this book. It is written for those who find themselves in a deeply passionate but "illicit" love affair, against every voice of reason and morality (perhaps including most of all their own), against every ounce of strength of will, against every impulse to self-preservation. It is intended as a survival guide, a map, a compass to use in unfamiliar terrain – the country of the newly passionate self in a deeply paradoxical situation.

There is a point of view here, but it is not one that would sew a scarlet letter on anyone's breast. It cautions every reader that if there is the slightest possibility of pulling back from the precipice, if it is at all possible that it is not too late, *stop*. Turn around and go home, and don't look back. If it is too late, you are on the verge of

falling into inner reaches of yourself that you have not
visited before and whose depths you have not yet
plumbed.

This exploration of love affairs prepares you and
accompanies you while you undertake this journey seriously and actively, and will help you begin to step aside
from some of the "passivity" that may have inflected
your passion and brought you to where you are today. It
offers you Ariadne's fine thread to find your way out of
the depths of your labyrinth and back out into the sun –
a form of "action" to balance "passion" and help you to
survive.

A Typical Beginning

A married woman in midlife steps casually into the
office of an acquaintance, a married male colleague, to
say hello. They have not seen each other in several years
due to their respective roles in their organization, and
are pleased to have a few minutes to catch up. Five minutes after delightedly shaking hands and beginning a
completely normal conversation, both are aware that the
atmosphere has subtly but distinctly changed. Eye contact is no longer simply an attentive courtesy; it is now a
searching, a probe.

The conversation continues but the pitch of their
voices has deepened, softened; the rhythm of their
speech has slowed. Their bodies sitting across the desk
from each other have stilled into a motionless waiting.
Soon there is a brief silence. Their eyes have become
openings into their souls, and each feels the terror of

letting the other see in – the first nakedness.

He breaks the silence. I can't offer you much, he says. She asks whether he can offer friendship. A few minutes after their initial handshake, the world has changed. For her, the old world is gone completely, in an instant, although she doesn't fully realize it yet. She will soon leave her husband and enter a disorienting new world that has only a tightrope across an abyss for footing. For him, his old world begins in these moments to coexist side by side with the new.

And for both of them, it is already too late to change their minds. The time to have given it up was the instant it was first offered – once that moment has passed and there has been a "yes," whether implied or explicit, it is immediately too late, forever; this is the sway that passion holds over imagination and longing.

I offer no judgements upon either him or her. Each will have to live with the consequences of the decisions that have now been made. However, the point of view of this exploration of love affairs is that no matter how nonjudgemental we are, the objective truth is that these can be extremely damaging relationships, and that it is very hard to either escape from or live with the suffering they create.

In fact, it can be said truthfully that such a love affair could very well be the most damaging kind of relationship there is. It is very difficult, even impossible, to defend yourself against love. How can you reject love, or the one who loves you, when there is no brutality or abuse, when your whole being responds to loving and being loved? And make no mistake: the love in these situations is very, very real. What makes love so damaging here is its context, a setting which brings with it complex social, structural, and dynamic elements that begin almost immediately to act on the participants in very harmful ways.

Typically, a love affair brings its participants a unique combination of intense pleasures and intense suffering, leading to important psychological consequences. This is particularly true for the unattached partner, if there is one. Some of these consequences take the form of extreme but conflicting emotions; others are cognitive, in the form of deeply held but also conflicting beliefs. A particularly difficult consequence is the special kind of isolation that is built into participation in a love affair. Ultimately these elements and others lead to the most devastating consequence of all, involving a kind of *fragmentation of the integrity of the personhood* of the partners, particularly an unattached partner, which is extremely damaging. It is too easy to dismiss such relationships as not serious or even pathological, and simply to advise the fragmented and bewildered individual to "get out." If it were that easy, our literature and drama, for example, would reflect that ease, our everyday experience would underscore it. Clearly it is not easy. What is needed most of all, it seems, before impatient dismissal and unreflective advice, is clarity – some sort of framework for understanding the conflicts and other phenomena uniquely associated with love affairs, guidelines that will indicate how to understand some of these conflicts, how to live with them, and also how to live without them.

Assumptions

I am working under several assumptions in contemplating the various dimensions of love affairs.

The first assumption is that this sort of relationship has always existed and always will exist; it is a fact of life that we all might find ourselves in such a situation at some time and that there are no moral judgements that need to be made here, because the emphasis is on understanding. This exploration neither "approves" nor "disapproves" of such a relationship, but it does try to clarify and explain it. The particular situation it addresses, however, is that of one who is *unattached* involved in a love affair with someone who is *married*. While many love affairs are arrangements made between two married persons, the fact that they are both married softens the fragmenting effects of living dual lives because of the very symmetry of the arrangement. Such partners, while perhaps experiencing deep emotional and cognitive dissonances between their marriages and their affair, nevertheless are spared the acutely and uniquely devastating effects of a love affair upon the unattached partner who must deal with a married lover.

The second assumption is that involvement in such a relationship does not necessarily mean that one is neurotic, evil, ignorant, or childlike in some way. Although these characteristics may indeed apply to one or the other partner in some relationships of this sort, to judge the partners in all love affairs automatically as pathological is a pop-psychology snap judgement made because it saves the trouble of thinking seriously about a complex and difficult issue. I assume a situation in which neither partner in the love affair is exploitative, cynical, neurotically dependent, or emotionally needy in some way. No one has necessarily been seduced, entrapped, manipulated, or otherwise psychologically coerced to take part; it is completely voluntary on the part of both people. I assume, in short, that both partners are rational, serious, competent, essentially moral and good-hearted adults who perhaps have found themselves overtaken by unexpected passion, have made choices about their lives because of this, and are prepared to accept responsibility for those choices. I also assume that it takes some courage on both sides to make this particular choice, especially in a moral and social climate that holds these sorts of relationships in severe contempt.

In relation to this, a third assumption I make is that the love that exists between the two people involved in a love affair is real love; that is to say, they are not mistaken about their real feelings and they are not deluding themselves. They are not "in love with love," nor are they merely erotically infatuated or using the affair to evade boredom. My assumption is that their relationship is based on a true and joyful recognition of the other *as a person* and that their erotic and intellectual passion is based firmly on that "I – Thou" recognition, the recognition of the Other not as alien, but as the *other self*. This is the reason for not examining affairs based on actual pathology or manipulation. The case in which there is genuine love is the most difficult one of all both to live with and to understand, since the self-protections of blaming, name-calling, and easy pop-psychology explanation are irrelevant and therefore not available. It is also paradoxically the most difficult one to justify – how can we explain permitting our genuinely loved partner to endure the pain of a secret, illicit love relationship? One must then look deeply into the nature of the actual relationship itself to search for clues to its profound mystery.

My fourth assumption is that the married partner does not wish to leave his or her spouse, for whatever reason. I assume that this partner is willing to conduct a love relationship with another person indefinitely, outside of the boundaries of his or her marriage. Once again, I do not make judgements about this decision. Moral judgements are easily available elsewhere; this exploration is not for that purpose.*

I also assume the perhaps controversial point that there are usually no innocent adult victims in the eternal triangle after it has been established for a period of time; everyone, including the uninvolved spouse, is more than likely to be complicit in whatever is occurring. If a marriage involves living together in the same residence, managing finances, household, children, and relatives together, and generally having intimate knowledge of and caring feelings for one another, then it necessarily requires some conscious or unconscious turning away from available evidence for the uninvolved spouse to continue to be "unaware" of an ongoing extramarital relationship. The only way such unawareness could conceivably be genuine is if the couple has long since stopped caring about each other and no longer pay attention, any attention, to what the other is doing. This, of course, excuses neither of the parties in the love affair

---

* However, as this meditation on love affairs progresses, facts will speak for themselves and may generate empathetic responses of one sort or another for the reader.

from their responsibility in building and perpetuating the lie that is lived in relation to the marriage.

These assumptions describe a life-situation and relationship that can be one of the most exciting and enriching in the world, but is at the same time one of the most intensely difficult and painful to endure. The difficulties faced by both partners have been vividly described and worked over by literature, drama, biography, and history for centuries, but they are worth looking at briefly again in simplified and undramatic form.

First, it is a relationship that is extremely difficult to sustain. The philosopher Richard Taylor and most other writers on the subject remind us that "affairs always end," that they are usually limited in duration.* This is normally true, but it is hard to reconcile with the intense emotion that is typically felt by both partners in the relationship, emotion that says "forever" and "only you." One of the primary reasons for the temporary nature of love affairs is usually a lack of understanding of what is expected by the other partner and what a love affair actually is. Once correct understanding is achieved, theoretically it can become possible to continue a love affair indefinitely, with minimal damage; "correct understanding," however, requires an intensity and acuity of self-discipline that is itself extremely difficult to sustain over time.

It is a relationship in which it is difficult to maintain perspective, because after a while it seems as though nothing is as it seems to be and one's mind seems always

---

* Richard Taylor, *Having Love Affairs*. (Buffalo, NY: Prometheus Books, 1990.)

to be playing tricks. Emotions are constantly on a roller-coaster ride, and thoughts seem permanently split between "on the one hand, on the other hand." This meditation on love affairs will offer some ways to clarify and focus thought and emotion in order to regain perspective and objectivity.

Most of all it is a relationship in which it is extraordinarily difficult to maintain a strong sense of self, because it takes place within a set of circumstances that easily foster personal fragmentation and a diminishing sense of self-esteem and self-respect, particularly for the unattached partner. At the same time, a strong sense of self is essential not only to survive such a relationship merely intact, but also to growing within it and emerging from it whole, integrated, and joyful to have had what can be an unforgettably rich experience.

These and other issues are the themes of this exploration aimed at understanding love affairs. It can be useful for both partners in the situation, but much of it is directed specifically toward the unattached partner. This is not because of any particular prejudice, but because given the essential nature of the relationship, the unattached partner is in a more confused and ambiguous position, suffering more deeply and seriously the effects of the love affair, and needing the most clarification. While it is true that the married partner typically also suffers deeply from the excruciating day-to-day compromises that become necessary when the decision is made to try to fulfill marital obligations while loving another, an important point to be noted is that it is precisely the married partner who can change the essential nature of the situation. The unmarried partner cannot.

Little or no attention is given here to the spouse of the married partner. This is not because the spouse's situation is not important, nor is it because the spouse is "complicit" in the triangle in the way suggested above. It is because this spouse's situation has already been given a great deal of attention, sympathy, and support. For example, many publications and books offer self-help advice for either holding on to a straying mate or surviving the aftermath of the mate's affair. Socially, furthermore, this spouse is the beneficiary of tremendous solidarity from almost all quarters; if the moral support provided is a bit patronizing, insisting as it does on the spouse's "victimization" as the price, nevertheless it is support and it is sympathy. And finally, in the cultural sphere, literature and film typically portray the spouse as unjustly betrayed and wronged, with the straying mate getting his or her well-deserved comeuppance in the end.

Surprisingly, perhaps, given the almost reflexive sympathy for the betrayed spouse, the married partners in the affair also have certain more subtle and less overt social and cultural supports available to them. If the straying spouse is male, for example, the supportive ideology is usually biological in nature, placing the male in an evolutionary context that asserts that it is somehow "unnatural" to expect monogamy and that the male is "expected" to scatter his seed liberally into suitable females in order to maintain the vigor of the species.* If

---

* E.g., *The Moral Animal*, by Robert Wright (NY: Vintage Books, 1994). Most people do not take in Mr. Wright's scattered admonitions that just because a behavior can be explained as "natural," it does not mean that it is also something that ought to be done.

the straying spouse is female, on the other hand, sympathetic female authors and researchers imply and support the permissibility of extramarital affairs on the grounds that passion, intimacy, and excitement are missing in the marriage – in other words, vibrant, talented, and passionate women in the prime of their lives should not be expected calmly to agree to be faithful to dull and unrewarding marriages. (It is also made clear, however, that these dull marriages and their accompanying material comforts are not to be given up.)*

The unattached partner has nothing comparably available to provide social or cultural support, and is in need of attention and a method for attaining clarity. This partner is routinely dismissed in serious literature and social intercourse as immoral, childlike, predatory, or pathological; there is little explanatory biological context within which to place this person,† nor is there a sympathetic understanding that his or her thwarted talents and passions need and, by implication ought to have, an outlet.

There is no assumption made here that the unattached partner is female and the married partner is male. Although this is the more typical pattern, single men do also find themselves involved with married women occasionally, and when that happens, they also experience all the confusion, suffering, and ambiguities of being in that position. Gay and lesbian love affairs may also run afoul of

---

* E.g., *The Erotic Silence of the American Wife*, by Dalma Heyn (NY: Random House, 1992); *Secret Loves*, by Sonya Friedman (NY: Crown Publishers, 1994).

† Mr. Wright provides one.

a previous serious and long-standing commitment on the part of one of the partners, for example if one of the partners is bisexual and is literally married to someone else.*

This is a book explicitly oriented toward understanding and surviving love affairs. It is written, as I said, primarily for the unattached partner, but there are insights available here for the married partner as well. Here are some of the areas which will be explored.

· Part I begins with a look at the Self as the first step in understanding this situation and regaining some control over it. We will examine why the integrity or wholeness of the Self, the person, is immediately vulnerable to the effects of being in a love affair and why it is the key element in trying to re-adjust some of these damaging and painful circumstances. Various written exercises will help the reader to begin to strengthen his or her Self or personhood as preparation for seeing clearly and deciding on appropriate action.

· Part II examines the nature of a love affair. Why is it that this particular kind of relationship, above all others, causes such a conflict of love and suffering, of values and ideas, and such tremendous overall confusion and disorientation? Is there any way to navigate within such a

---

* The special kind of secrecy that gay or lesbian lovers face under these circumstances may involve particularly painful kinds of suffering-in-isolation and a multi-leveled social withholding of acknowledgement that include all the suffering of heterosexual secret affairs, and then some. A complete exploration of these issues is unfortunately beyond the reach of these explorations, but some of the meditations and exercises offered here will certainly be applicable and, I hope, helpful.

relationship so that one is not trapped by these conflicts and ambiguities? It will become clear that this is, in fact, possible. Written exercises in this section are oriented toward separating truth from illusion.

· Part III explores the nature of sex and lovemaking and shows the importance of how time operates in love affairs, as well as in daily life. Time plays special kinds of tricks on persons in love affairs, especially fostering absorption in memories and stereotypes on the one hand, and in anticipations and expectations on the other hand. Under these circumstances there is little space available to be actually present in the real moment that is taking place now, but paradoxically (and cruelly), the only moment that is typically available to the partners in a love affair *is* the present moment. This section shows why the "here-and-now" has such tremendous importance in this relationship in particular, and also for life in general. The exercises here are geared toward developing an orientation to the present and how correctly to assess what living in the here-and-now actually amounts to.

· Part IV is concerned with actually making choices and making changes. There are typically three rational options available for the unattached partner in this situation – one that involves leaving the affair, two others that can allow it to continue. This section also discusses different kinds of love and offers guidelines for intimacy, ethics, etiquette, and friendship within the parameters of this special kind of relationship. The final exercise shows how to tap into a creative "inner voice," what the philosopher Socrates used to call his "mantic voice" – the voice that can help in making conscious, creative decisions and choices about complex and difficult life issues.

It is important to note here that this manual does not pretend to know all the questions, to provide all the answers, or to relieve all the suffering. Often, especially when a love affair is in its beginning stages, the intensity and range of emotion are overwhelming – ecstatic and agonizing in dizzying alternation, or sometimes simultaneously. Under those circumstances, a calm and objective exploration of the situation may seem irrelevant and unhelpful, while not addressing the need for immediate relief. However, these explorations and exercises are not structured to offer immediate emotional relief, nor to give final answers to all questions. They are intended, rather, to provide a method for self-exploration and analysis that makes a beginning, that can allow one to take the first steps toward self-understanding and strength, to bring out the inner voice.

1
Anatomy of the Self

How does an affair begin? It is likely that it begins with joy. Suddenly you find yourself in a situation that is charged with romance, passion, and mystery; you feel deep intimacy and fulfillment, perhaps for the first time. With joy and relief, you allow yourself to become completely involved and immersed, perhaps even against your own better judgement. You experience a complete engagement and absorption of your Self in all its dimensions: emotional, intellectual, sexual, spiritual. From your lover, you experience complete reinforcement of all these parts of you – finally, you think, someone really understands how to love you. The relationship itself seems to nurture and support all these aspects of your being and the "fit" is so perfect you may feel as though you have known your lover forever. Montaigne speaks of "souls that mingle and blend with each other so completely that they efface the seam that joined them, and cannot find it again."[*] In short, you are deeply in love and your lover is obviously deeply in love with you. The mutual awareness of each other's love is even more thrilling and enhances passion and its intimacy even more. You are riding on a cloud of ecstasy that carries you through your days and nights in a way that is unimaginably sublime and filled with the sweetness of fulfilled passion.

Typically, there eventually comes a moment that jolts you rudely out of your dream world. Perhaps, while you are speaking on the telephone of something important to you, your lover hangs up on you abruptly because his or her spouse has entered the room. Later it is reasonably explained to you that it had to be done, that it was necessary and unavoidable. Your immediate response may have been shame and anger, but you feel you must also acknowledge the reasonableness of the explanation. However, your shame and anger remain, in spite of reason. At another time, your lover may casually inform you that he or she is going on a scheduled two-week vacation trip with his or her spouse – to Paris, to the Caribbean, to Italy, to New Orleans, to Disney World. There appears to be an assumption that of course you will understand the necessity of these sorts of events, and there is a matter-of-fact expectation that you will continue the relationship in spite of them. You are expected to agree that from time to time you may be hung up on; from time to time you must sit and wait at home for your lover to come back from vacation. These

---

[*] Michel de Montaigne, "Of Friendship," in Michael Pakaluk, *Other Selves: Philosophers on Friendship* (Indianapolis, IN: Hackett Publishing Company, Inc., 1991).

things are necessary and are part and parcel of the relationship as it is. These are the first overt blows to the integrity of your Self – typically there are many more to come.

"Integrity" here refers literally to "wholeness," to the quality of being complete and unimpaired. The events and situations just described force you into a special kind of fragmentation of your Self that specifically opposes integrity because it divides you into pieces. How are you to respond to the imperative that although the person you love is going on a two-week vacation with his or her spouse, you are expected not to show or even feel hurt and anger because you understand the necessity of the trip? How can you assent to having your lover hang up on you and swallow your feelings of anger and shame on the grounds of understanding? If you are to accept these imperatives, it will require the splitting of your Self into the part that feels, and the part that tries to talk you out of feeling. Ultimately, assenting to these and other circumstances will leave you feeling powerless and diminished in self-esteem. Simultaneously, you are still feeling the joys and fulfillments of the deepest passion and love you have perhaps ever known; your feelings of hurt, shame, and anger must be experienced side-by-side with your intense emotional engagement with this magical love you have found – more fragmentation. Your emotional being is divided from itself and from your rational being; your rational being is struggling to see the world through your lover's eyes and your own perspective seems somehow flawed or incomplete. Eventually, you might just give up the struggle in resignation, depression, and exhaustion.

These injuries are not deliberately inflicted on you by

your lover in order to cause you suffering; it is fair to say that if your lover has real feelings for you, he or she is genuinely distressed by your pain and feels genuinely guilty and responsible for it. The truth is, however, that these kinds of injuries come with this package; they are part and parcel of such a relationship. If you have experienced them, remember that you are not alone; if they have not yet happened, they will. In Part 2 of this series of explorations, you will see why this is so and what you can do about it. For now, let us start at the beginning by examining your self and why it is so important to be "self-centered" for now.

The Self

The analysis of what actually constitutes "self" or "personhood" is endlessly controversial and consumes volumes of philosophy, psychology, sociology, and anthropology. These analyses are not just abstract; how we constitute personhood has serious implications for public policy in law, medicine, education, religion, and government, to name only a few areas. For the purposes of this discussion, let us use this concept in its everyday understanding: your Self is both your outer and your inner person, and we can understand that person in a common-sense way by contemplating some of its responsibilities and activities in the world.

Your "outer" person takes care of your public life: your professional, work, or business obligations; your personal relationships – friends, parents, siblings, children, spouse, lover; and your citizenship in your community, your society, and the world at large. Your "inner" person, on the other hand, takes care of your private life: it takes care of your body by maintaining its physical health, and it takes care of your soul, or psyche, by attending to your emotional, mental, and spiritual health.*

Your "person," both outer and inner – your *self* – operates at its best in your world by being capable of *taking effective action* in all these areas. But what is effective action, and why is it so vital when considering the responsibilities and activities of the outer and inner person?

Effective Action

"Action" means being in motion, doing something; "effective" means producing a desired result. "Effective action" therefore means moving through your life and doing things which by and large have results that you desire and that you can foresee. This can be broken down into two broad functional areas of life and living.

The ability and willingness to act *intelligently, rationally, and in an informed way* requires being capable of analyzing a situation more or less correctly, having the ability and imagination to handle the situation by "rehearsing" mentally several courses of action while having a general sense of the consequences of each, and subsequently being decisive by choosing and then carrying out one of the courses of action you have contemplated. Of course, analysis of a situation and rehearsing

---

* " 'Psyche' is the soul – a term full of the richest meaning, endowed with emotion, comprehensively human and unscientific." From Bruno Bettelheim's *Freud and Man's Soul* (NY: Vintage Books, 1984).

courses of action do not necessarily take place in the linear, formal, step-by-step procedure that these terms imply; this depends on one's personal style and temperament. The point is that one must experience being "present" to the various aspects of a situation in some conscious way that permits understanding and effective decision-making to take place. Being decisive also does not necessarily imply an aggressive or single-minded pursuit of goals; the main issue is the ability to choose and then the will to act on that choice.

The other area of effective action requires the ability and willingness to act *compassionately, empathetically, and in a concerned and engaged way* in your relationships with others – in other words, you are willing and able to step aside from your own interests, step into another person's shoes, and take another person's interests to heart. This also requires having the capacity and willingness to analyze situations, rehearse courses of action, and know consequences, but this time *from the other person's point of view* – having, in short, the ability to experience empathy. This allows you to be able to give empathetic support or wise advice, to know the difference between the two, and also to have increased tolerance and understanding for others and for their life circumstances. This is a way of understanding what it means to be compassionate, and it tends toward rational peace-making in your world rather than toward mindless, aggressive bickering.

When the parts of your Self are not integrated – when your personhood has "dis-integrated" or lost its wholeness – some or all of these rational and emotional capabilities typically are affected negatively, and so is your active interest in the activities and responsibilities of your world. Poor thinking may compromise your business, work, or professional decisions; these may be made impulsively without the patience to analyze situations or rehearse consequences; perhaps they are even delayed indefinitely, making you tentative and indecisive. Moreover, your personal relationships may be adversely affected by your inability or unwillingness to step out of your own world and into the worlds of others; perhaps you become impatient, dismissive, intolerant; you may ignore the legitimate needs and desires of others because you don't have sufficient emotional energy to focus on them.

A love affair can cause just these kinds of fragmentation and "dis-integration" of the self that subsequently interfere with your effective presence in your world. As we began to see above, it can set your emotions at war with themselves and against your reason. Your powerful feelings, both favorable and unfavorable, may be in constant confrontation with your strong beliefs, both pro and con. Your reason itself is probably divided as you try to jockey between your lover's point of view and your own, which are in direct conflict with each other much of the time.

Other Causes of Fragmentation

If you imagine your *relationship* having an "inner" and "outer" aspect, just as you do as a *person*, you may find these inner and outer parts of your relationship are at odds with one another as well.

In the first place, you will have to reconsider the ordinary meanings of commonplace ideas that you thought you understood very well. One such concept is "love"; what does "love" mean from inside your relationship? What does it mean outside? Normally, we understand that deep feelings of love bring certain consequences with them – usually, at least an open and public change in one's life as room is made for the loved person in one's daily activities. In a typical love affair, no such change is or can be made openly. Although we may certainly alter our daily schedules to perhaps include a regular lunch or coffee break with our lover, it is significant that this must be done without fully acknowledging the true nature of the relationship publicly. Does this mean that our love isn't real, or does it mean that we don't in fact understand love the way we thought we did? There are other conundrums as well, regarding such concepts as "trust," "fidelity," "obligation," and so on – you are likely to need two conceptual languages for such ideas instead of only one. Many previously-understood concepts are going to have to be reconsidered if they are to be applicable to your relationship; you have begun the process of inhabiting two sometimes very different realities at the same time. At the same time that old meanings still hold sway outside of your relationship, inside there is a new vocabulary and a new standard of significance that must be learned, sometimes painfully.

Another area of confusion is morality. What is your duty, and to whom? Is it your cosmic duty to love where you find love, or is it your more local duty to follow the moral guidelines of your community or society? Can these be made compatible with each other? Do you, the unattached partner, have any responsibilities to the betrayed spouse? Do you, the straying spouse, have responsibilities of fidelity to your husband or wife? How is fidelity to be understood? *Is* the spouse "betrayed"? Duties, obligations, and responsibilities are ideas that are closely connected to love and friendship and which generally operate fairly clearly in ordinary relationships; in love affairs, however, these ideas are initially very murky and must be re-examined and perhaps turned upside down. Again, in order to participate in your love affair, you might need two systems of understanding obligation, responsibility, and duty instead of only one.

A third area of difficulty is social. How do you reconcile having an important personal love relationship with the fact that society almost universally dislikes and disapproves of it (at least officially and publicly)? How do you deal with your need to share your joy or your pain, knowing you cannot really speak freely about it? Again, there is fragmentation, this time in regard to the need for living a vital part of your life hidden from view. This separates your personal life from your social life in a way that makes no bridges even theoretically possible. You will literally have to live a dual life.

Psychological Consequences of Fragmentation

All these causes of fragmentation and dis-integration leave potentially damaging psychological consequences in their wake. For example, you may begin to feel disoriented when you realize that words don't always have their normal meaning. "Disorientation" means exactly what it says – your position in relation to the various elements of ordinary life changes so dramatically that you will need time to readjust, and in fact you may never readjust. You may continue fighting to have words mean what you think they mean, and then demand that your lover assent to those meanings and act upon them as you understand them. This is a fertile cause of hostility and misunderstanding in an already difficult situation. If you do understand the need for two separate meaning systems, you nevertheless still have to maintain your old orientation to these same elements when you are dealing with your outside relationships and with your ordinary life. You may end up feeling very confused and unsure of your understanding as you struggle with adopting these varying perspectives.

The tremendously important moral issues involved in having love affairs are another potential source of destructive psychological effects. You may have always thought of yourself as a moral person; now you may not be so sure. Regardless of what television and popular culture may tell us, it really is not true that people yearn to be involved in these sorts of relationships. They may desire passion and romance, but not actually in this context. Most people disapprove of extramarital affairs, and you may have been one of them before you got involved in this one. You may even have had serious and justifiable moral attitudes of disapproval toward love affairs – disapproval of the deceptive and secretive aspects of them, for example – but now, here you are, acting against every belief and moral value you had held and perhaps expressed earlier. How are you supposed to think about yourself now? This is not only disorienting, but as you continue in your affair without acting upon your sincere previous beliefs, this may lead to a further erosion of self-esteem and a change for the worse in your understanding of yourself.

An associated element in the eventual erosion of self-respect may come paradoxically from consideration of your voluntary participation in the affair. Though your lover claims to love only you, you have a growing awareness of your second-class and incidental status in your lover's life, which is so just by the nature of things, and you are aware that *you are allowing it to be this way*. It is pitifully true that there is really no reason for you to have to endure any of this – all you need to do is to walk away. Of course, this is much easier said than done, but even recognizing that does not change your knowledge that you are in this under your own steam. The knowledge that your participation is completely voluntary, combined with an apparent inability or unwillingness to leave such a painful and damaging situation, can and often does cause a tremendous loss of self-respect – something that divides you from your good opinion of yourself.

A very stressful consequence of fragmentation is that various "pieces" of you feel different things at the same time, causing you to experience your emotions as extremely incoherent and conflicted. They are intense and uncontrollable and give you a daily steep roller coaster ride from intense ecstasy to intense misery and back again in the space of a very short time. Moreover, they often seem to be in direct conflict with each other – how can you both love deeply and resent bitterly the same person at the same time? How can you feel both intense joy and powerful anger simultaneously? This conflict and incoherence of emotions is not just a consequence of being "in pieces," but also over time becomes itself a cause of even more internal fragmentation.

It is easy to see now why it is extremely important to focus on your Self at the beginning of these explorations. It is your actual self – your personhood – that is being fragmented and undermined by all these circumstances and elements. Over time, you are likely to begin experiencing increasing mental fatigue, emotional exhaustion, and spiritual resignation. The stress response eventually sets in with depression and learned helplessness, since there doesn't seem to be anything you can do to help yourself, either in or out of your relationship. This is often combined with rage, hostility, shame, and other deeply unpleasant feelings. Whatever happened to joy, love, passion, and intimacy? Incredibly, they are still there; this is what it actually means to say that all these emotions must be experienced side by side.

The overall effect may be a massive change in you from a person *acting* effectively and coherently in the world to one *reacting* passively and irrationally to events and feelings that do not fit into a unified and coherent framework that you can understand. From our earlier reflections on effective action and on the causes and effects of fragmentation, you can begin to see the condition of your psyche, your soul. What you are likely to see is that it is disorganized and jumbled, somewhat incoherent, and very "noisy" as conflicting thoughts and conflicting emotions jostle one another for your attention. Your ability to act effectively is compromised, and it is tempting to look at the fact of your voluntary participation as somehow implying that it is all your fault, after all, for agreeing to such a situation in the first place. This, of course, further reinforces the erosion of self-respect we spoke about earlier.

The slowly dawning, bitter truth of the matter, the part that must be looked at closely and carefully, is that the situation is not going to change by itself, and neither will your lover. This is the key – recognizing that unless your situation is one of the rare ones, typically it is going to stay the same until and unless you change it. Short of actually withdrawing from it altogether, the only way you can even think about changing it is to strengthen yourself by understanding clearly what you are facing, recognizing your own fragmentation, and beginning the work of re-integrating yourself into a whole person. It is the whole person who will be able once again to take effective action in the world, to be consciously present to the varying aspects of complex situations, to take another person's point of view appropriately. You will be in charge of your own life again, and you will once again be able to make responsible, rational, compassionate decisions. This will increase your self-esteem, restore your self-respect, and improve your self-image. As you are restored, your capacity for rational action and empathetic relationships will strengthen, and your decision-making in relation to your affair will be improved.

Taking Steps

Sometimes just knowing that someone else is aware of how we feel is all that is needed. Perhaps just by reading these explorations and learning the hidden dynamics of uncommon love relationships you may get a sense of the directions that you need to take, and that knowledge will inspire you to go ahead and take the actions that seem indicated. For those who are interested, this series of explorations offers several powerful written and/or contemplative exercises that will allow you to achieve satisfying resolutions of some of the more complex issues. To write these exercises, you will need a notebook; for either writing or contemplation, you will need a strong desire to understand yourself and your life again, and the commitment to follow through (in short, to begin acting effectively by deciding to do these exercises, and then actually doing them.)

Most of these exercises work best as written, journal-type meditations, but they may be done in a non-written, contemplative manner as well. Each method has its advantages and disadvantages, but I strongly recommend doing them as written exercises. For one thing, their effects are more powerful when they are written. The physical act of writing things down reinforces the mental and emotional work that is being done, and furthermore writing necessarily slows down thought so that one typically thinks more clearly and more deeply when writing. This is also why I recommend writing by hand rather than using a computer or a typewriter. Moreover, when deeply engaged in personal exploration through writing, often one finds oneself writing things that are unexpected – perhaps some novel connection has been made between elements of a situation, or a previously unnoticed aspect of a problem comes to the surface. Such writings are from the unconscious part of the person and their surprising manifestations are more likely to occur while hand-writing rather than using a keyboard.

Finally, the effects of doing self-exploratory work last longer when the work is written. Besides the reinforcing effects of hand-writing, there is also a record that can be revisited for review and contemplation; in the months and years to come, various patterns become evident, which can add perspective not only to one's past but to the present as well. It is also easier to track changes in oneself, providing powerful reinforcement as one becomes stronger. Finally, a record of this rich life-giving and important work is extremely valuable for its own sake.

However, your time may be short, so you may choose to do this work as a series of contemplative exercises. This will provide a more intense experience in the moment and a more rapid progress through the exercises, but unless you are already experienced in meditative or contemplative techniques, you may find yourself too easily distracted by extraneous thoughts, outside noises, and so on. However, there is nothing stopping you from doing them many times over as contemplative work, thereby getting a more textured and multi-layered experience over time. If you choose to work through these exercises without writing, it is important to set aside both an adequate amount of time (not less than an hour) and a quiet, reasonably noise-free space where you are not subject to being interrupted by telephone, children, or anything else. In addition, you will need a comfortable chair to sit in, if you cannot or choose not to use traditional meditative postures on the floor. It is not advisable to lie down, since the physical relaxation that typically attends prolonged meditation will make it easy simply to fall asleep. These exercises require undivided and focused attention, and not a dreamy, fuzzy, pre-sleep mental state.

Exercises 1 and 2 are deceptively simple and may appear at first glance too obvious to take very seriously;

however, they are the groundwork for the rest of the dozen exercises in this book, so it is extremely important that you take the time to do them thoroughly and carefully. Their importance may only be appreciated after they are done seriously and in good faith; you will understand yourself a good deal better for having done them carefully and in detail.

In order to begin to understand how you actually experience the condition of your personhood, how its condition right now is affecting you and your life, and how you can begin to rebuild and strengthen yourself in order to change your life, it is essential to go back into your life before you began your love affair. This is going to require you to take an imaginative trip back into your memory and to steep yourself in who you were "before."

A note about writing if you are anxious about it – *no one is going to see your writing except you,* unless you give your permission. This means do not worry about grammar, syntax, spelling, punctuation, or good handwriting. It also means don't edit your ideas because you think they might be unacceptable in some way. If they are your real ideas, they deserve to see the light of day. Just write, and let your ideas flow without editing.

Exercise 1

Re-acquaintance with your old self.
{May take anywhere from 1 hour to several days.}

This is an exercise that asks the question: who were you

in the months and weeks immediately before beginning your love affair? Go back approximately to the 6-month period prior to beginning your relationship with your lover. What was your old self like? It is important to be able to describe yourself "back then" with as much clarity and accuracy as possible; this gives you a clear picture to compare with who you are today. By the way, the effectiveness of this exercise does not depend upon how long ago you began your affair; you are likely to be a changed person whether it started 6 months or 6 years ago.

- List all your **physical characteristics** as you remember them. Pull out an old snapshot if your memory needs some help. Use specific adjectives to describe yourself, as if you were trying to describe yourself to someone who doesn't know you. Be vivid and concrete: height, weight, hair color and style, style of dress, the condition of your health, and so on.

- What was your **daily life** like? What did you eat? How often? How long did you sleep? Did you sleep well? Did you have a sex life? What was it like? With whom? If not, how long had it been since you had had sex? What did you do on your weekends? What kind of books did you like to read? What were your favorite television shows, movies, magazines? Any hobbies?

- What was your general **feeling tone**? Were you calm, anxious, content, satisfied, unsatisfied, depressed, ambitious, cheerful, bored, energetic? Were you jumpy, relaxed, irritable, mellow, serene, grouchy, silly? Did you feel competent, that you had a sense of mastery over most areas of your life? Did you feel helpless or overwhelmed much of the time? Again, be specific and concrete.

- What were your **accomplishments, achievements,**

projects? What sort of work did you do? Did you have a job? Did you like it? Why or why not? Did you have chil-dren? Were you a good parent?

▪ What were your **desires, ambitions, dreams, fears, anxieties, hopes**? Talk about them in detail, using as much time as is required to give an accurate picture. What did you hope to accomplish in work, in love, in personal growth? What were you afraid of? What kind of life did you dream of for yourself? What were your fantasies about? Money? Love? Power?

▪ Did you have any **vices**? Cigarettes, alcohol, drugs, overeating? Addictions to sex, gambling, overwork, choco-late? How did you feel about these practices?

▪ What about **friendships** and participation as a citizen in your community? Were your friendships intimate or casu-al? What was it about yourself that steered you either toward or away from intimacy with your friends? Did you do any volunteer work? What kind? Did you like it? Were you good at it?

▪ Did you have a **spiritual practice** or **religious faith**? If so, what was your relationship to it? Did it satisfy you? Did you satisfy its ideals?

▪ Did you **like yourself** back then? Why or why not? Spend some time thinking about this carefully; this is the main question of the exercise. Note: the question is not whether today you like who you were then; that comes later. At the time, what did you feel about yourself? Try to guard against false modesty or false inflation here; it is important for you to be clear about who you actually were and how you felt about yourself and to record it without hiding virtues or varnishing vices.

At any time, go back and fill in what has occurred to you along the way as you handled a question and moved on to the next one.

An alternative form of this exercise would be simply to sit down and begin writing the narrative of your Self in that period preceding your affair, starting anywhere, and talking about the things that arise for you in your consciousness as you write. This is not, by the way, a "simpler" form of the exercise, since you are asked to be as concrete, detailed, and vivid in your descriptions as before. The difference is that you will choose your starting point and work onward from there in a less structured and systematic way.

Exercise 2

Now what about your present self?
{Again, may take anywhere from 1 hour to several weeks.}

It is best to wait a day or so after completing Exercise 1 before starting with Exercise 2. This will allow your mind to clear and re-focus on today. Do the same exercise again, in the same detail, only this time focus on describing yourself in the present day.

▪ Go over your physical and emotional characteristics today, using concrete, vivid adjectives. Have you changed? For the better or the worse? Both? What specific things about you have changed?

▪ Is your daily life different today in significant ways?

▪ Describe your activities and work. Also note whether you achieved any of the dreams and desires you described in the first exercise, and describe in detail what dreams and hopes you have today. Are they the same? Have they changed?

▪ What, if anything, have you done about your **vices**? Have you conquered any of them? Have you picked up some new ones, or re-connected with ones you had conquered before?

▪ Has your **spiritual or religious practice** changed? Do you now have one where you didn't before, or have you abandoned a practice that you did have?

▪ Most important, describe **how you feel about yourself** today, given the changes that have occurred in your life. Once again, try to be objective: no false modesty, no false inflation. The only way to get deeply into this exercise is to be completely honest. Remember, no one is going to see what you have written without your permission.

Comments:

These exercises may seem trivial and you may be impatient with them – after all, you probably feel as if you already know who you are and also who you were in the past. The truth is that it is usually not that easy to know who we are or were, and it does require careful thought. This is because of the tendency of the mind to simplify things. Simplifying our perceptions and memories is an efficiency mechanism which allows us to store information and knowledge more easily and in greater quantity. If we had to maintain active, conscious memory of every detail of our lives we would simply not be able to do so and a great deal of knowledge would be lost. However, the other side of the coin is that we may forget that each simplified idea is actually a kind of shorthand for more complex and detailed knowledge. Doing these exercises in good faith allows you to excavate what you *really* know about yourself but perhaps haven't thought about or thought through for a long time. You will locate things within yourself that you have forgotten or simply haven't given any thought to, as well as new pieces of knowledge about yourself that you were not aware of.

Exercise 3

Knowing How You Feel and What You Think
{Again, wait a day or two before you do this third exercise.}

▪ Read over what you wrote in Exercises 1 and 2 without interruption from beginning to end, and first, immediately write what you feel. Notice I don't say to write what you think. What do you feel? You don't need complete sentences, and it's important not to think too deeply about this part of the exercise. Just write the words that name your feelings, quickly, before you can think about them and edit them. If you feel bad, say so, and try to name the specific bad feelings. If you feel good, say that too, and also name those feelings. Your aim here is to contrast your "then" and "now" selves, which you have described vividly and concretely, and to react to the contrast.

Comments:
If your feelings are generally bad – depression, hostility,

anger, disappointment, sadness, regret, and so on – this is important information for you about yourself, and it is the starting point for change and growth. Again, don't blame yourself, but do take responsibility for recognizing the truth about your feelings toward yourself today.

If what you feel is generally good – excited, pleased, happy, satisfied, and so on – one of two things is probably true: either you don't need these explorations and exercises, because you have done your life right and it's turned out the way you want it, or you are "in denial." It is up to you to decide which of these two possibilities is the correct one. ("Denial" is a means by which one protects oneself from an unpleasant reality by unconsciously refusing to perceive or to face it. This is a defense mechanism which typically relieves tension and anxiety.)

After you write what you feel, shift gears and come back more into your head.

▪ Now write your **thoughts, ideas, and opinions** about the contrast between your "then" and "now" selves that has emerged from doing these two exercises. What do you think? Your thoughts don't have to be systematic and orderly – just write them down as they come to you. Maybe you are someone who thinks in pictures rather than words, so write down or even draw the images that come to you. How do you "see" yourself and the results of these exercises? Does what you think or what you "see" make sense? Is it confused and incoherent, or are your ideas clear and rational? Do you "see" clearly or are you in a kind of fog? Do you **know** what you think? Do you **have** any images?

▪ What are the most important contrasts between then and now that you noted? In what way are they important?

Comments:

Again, assess your thoughts and/or images in general. If they are confused, foggy, incoherent, jumbled, and so on, this again is important information and a starting point for change and growth. If your ideas and images are clear and coherent, if you know what you think and your ideas and opinions are generally favorable to yourself and your situation, then either you really don't need this series of meditations and exercises other than for your general interest, or once again you are in denial. You decide.

Now that you have done all this intense written or contemplative work, what does it all mean? Just this. You now have a pretty good idea of the condition of your "now" self, your person, your being-in-the-world, in contrast to your "then" self. You can name your feelings more or less accurately, you have an idea what your thinking is like, and you have a general sense of whether you feel mostly bad or mostly good about yourself.

As I said, if you feel mostly good about yourself, these explorations might be interesting for you, but you are not going to need them to help you. You seem to have already helped yourself pretty well. On the other hand, if you feel generally bad about your life, and I assume that is the more common outcome, don't despair. It is important to be able to describe yourself to yourself honestly and fairly. Knowing yourself is the first step toward growth and change.

Now that you have all this knowledge about yourself, what do you actually do with it? It is easy to say "try not to be depressed or upset about what these exercises told you about yourself and your life." That is about as useful as telling you not to feel pain when you hit your thumb with a hammer. Instead, I am going to put it slightly differently, and maybe this will surprise you. I am going to advise you to "try not to take it personally." What could this possibly mean? You may wonder how you are supposed to live through an intensely personal love affair, then do deeply personal exercises, and "not take it personally." I will explain.

There are going to be times when you are reading these explorations, doing these exercises, or living your life, for that matter, when you will have to be deeply within yourself and experience things intensely from the inside out – "taking it personally." But at the same time, it is important to begin trying to take yourself out of yourself and seeing yourself objectively and unemotionally from the outside in. This means that you have to start calling forth something called your "Observing Self." The Observing Self is that part of you which can detach itself from your immediate emotional, mental, and physical circumstances to "observe," dispassionately and objectively, the rest of you going through your life. It is an essential part of you – that which is left over after you take away most things characteristic of you and your world. It is the ability to feel what you feel, think what you think, and yet still maintain clear vision and perspective about that person who is you thinking and feeling in your own life. It is a kind of dual perspective that allows you to step away from emotion and your personal circumstances and take a detached point of view that is objective, unemotional, and unprejudiced. It is this Observing Self that is going to take you through this time of your life and that will help you in many other areas of your life as well. It is the clear "you" that is uncontaminated by confusion, disorientation, depression, or hostility.

This brings us to Exercise 4, developed from ancient traditions to allow recognition of the Observing Self.

Exercise 4

Your Observing Self
{This is a contemplative, not a written exercise.}

Sit quietly and comfortably, with your eyes closed if you like, and think about some of the words or phrases you used to describe your present self in Exercise 2. These descriptions are unique for the person who is you – they do not describe anyone else with exactly the same combination of qualities. In this exercise, you are going to try temporarily to "disconnect" these descriptions from yourself, one by one, and then examine what is left. Specifically, you will ask yourself, after each "disconnection," whether the person who is you is still there, and whether you have changed in your essential being. The idea is that all the physical, emotional, mental, and other qualities that together uniquely describe you are in some sense "accidental" – for example, if you have dark hair, you could just as well have been born with light hair and still be "you." If you are a computer programmer, you could just as well have chosen to be a concert pianist or a plumber and you would still be "you."

• For this exercise, sit quietly with your eyes closed, and begin by thinking of the description of your **outer, public**

life. You described work that you do, friends and colleagues that you have, and your family and relatives, among other things. One by one, "drop" these things from your description of yourself. If you did not have the particular work that you have, would you still be "you?" If you didn't have those particular friends, would you still be "you?" What about your family? Could they have been different, and would you still be "you" in that case?

▪ Next, take away all the **physical characteristics** that make you uniquely identifiable in the world. "Disconnect" your hair color, your height and weight, the color of your eyes, even your gender. Ask yourself after each disconnection whether "you" still exist, whether "you" are still there. You will find that you are. If you continue to separate your physical characteristics from your actual self, you will find that you can in fact, separate yourself from your entire physical being, and "you" will still be there (otherwise who is doing all this thinking?).

▪ Now begin to move inward, and do the same with your **emotions,** your **ambitions, dreams, desires, fantasies, fears, and anxieties**. This is even more difficult, but reflect that your emotions and all the rest are as "accidental" and therefore theoretically changeable as your physical characteristics. Your fantasies about power and prestige could just as well have been fantasies about being spiritually enlightened or artistically talented. If you change or eliminate these emotions, dreams, and fantasies, are "you" still there? Of course.

You begin to get the idea. The surprising thing about this is that you can take away everything that uniquely defines you and generates your feelings and ideas, but "you" are still there, thinking, doing this exercise. And this is the important part: you can still think, even though everything else that generates your passions and emotions is separated from you or altered in imagination. As you see, this understanding of the "essential you" can have a significant effect on your handling of the immediately pressing issues of your life.

Comments:

This is an ancient spiritual exercise used in meditation practices in various traditions, both Eastern and Western. The purpose of it is specifically to "separate" the so-called real, essential person from his or her particular circumstances in the world. The idea is that this real, essential person will be able to develop and grow spiritually, but only if he or she is separated from the distractions of the physical world. These distractions include especially one's own emotional and psychological states. Therefore, the "you" who is still there after the other characteristics are removed is not the "you" who is undergoing passion, emotion, and the joys and difficulties of daily life. The remaining, essential "you" has been stripped of these distractions in order to be able to think clearly and objectively about your life.

The exercise was developed in slightly different form and for different purposes by the great Enlightenment philosopher René Descartes. In his work **Meditations** he brought himself through the various stages of a similar exercise and ended by recognizing that because he thinks, he exists, even though he has thought himself "out" of the entire world. The famous saying "I think, therefore I am" is from Descartes. Although the Buddha took this exercise much farther than Descartes 2200 years earlier, for our purposes it is the clear, *thinking* self that we want to separate from the turmoil of everyday life, and it is this self that we want to call upon to assist us. It is this ability to think yourself out of your circumstances that evokes what is called in some traditions the Observing Self, and it is your Observing Self that will allow you eventually to pick up the true threads of your life and gradually become whole again.

For now, this exercise can begin to allow you to start strengthening the Observing Self in you. It is important to understand what I mean here. I am not suggesting that you aim for not feeling anything at all. That would not only be impossible, but also undesirable. You don't want to turn into an emotional zombie just because you don't want to feel pain. What is required is that at the same time you are feeling whatever it is you are feeling, you let your Observing Self step "outside" of you and simply observe you. Let your Observing Self dispassionately describe and identify what you are going through – feeling bad because of so-and-so; feeling confused and disoriented because of not understanding this or that; feeling rejected because something happened, or because nothing happened – and so on.

The events of everyday life provide more than enough opportunity to practice this movement from inside yourself to outside yourself. By practicing unemotionally describing and identifying what your psychological and physical self is doing and feeling, you will notice that a number of very interesting things will begin to happen. Gradually, you will find that you are not afraid of your conflicting emotions or confused thoughts any more. There is something wonderful about allowing yourself to feel what you feel and having your Observing Self simply tell you what that is. As you allow the Observing Self to speak to you, to tell you simply what you are feeling and to tell it with distance and objectivity, the feelings themselves will change. Over time they will lose their depth and sharpness and begin to fade. They will become gradually more manageable and ultimately almost unimportant.

Often, people in love affairs report being troubled by an inability to think clearly or act reasonably. If you have found yourself experiencing something similar, your Observing Self will allow you to distance yourself from feeling disturbed by it, merely by continuing dispassionately to observe you thinking and acting in your ongoing life by naming and identifying these problems. Once again, over time, your thoughts will begin to clear because of the distance provided by the Observing Self and you will begin to gain a more accurate perspective on things and on yourself.

Soon, you will find yourself automatically "switching over" as soon as you begin to feel "that" feeling or think "those" thoughts. You will begin to achieve a corrected perspective on your life, and that is a major step toward reaching your goal of being emotionally independent, strong, integrated, and whole. At the same time, your emotions will also begin to correct themselves and become more authentic – sadness, for example, instead of depression. You do not need to distance yourself from these authentic feelings, and in fact, you shouldn't. These are genuine expressions of your essential and unique humanity, and ought to be valued as part of the texture of your fully-lived life.

Eventually, you will find yourself beginning to act effectively in the world again, both in your business or work activities and in your personal relationships with your friends and loved ones. Your Self – your person – will become re-integrated and you will be able to continue strengthening yourself and living the full life you deserve, regardless of the circumstances. However, it is important to note that this requires a steady commitment to developing the Observing Self in your life. Merely doing this exercise once or twice will not alleviate all your pain and will not make the detached Observer instantly available to you. As an initial step, it will allow you some respite from suffering; with this partial relief, you may find the serenity and the energy to seek out other strengthening techniques for yourself, such as meditation, exercise, art, community service, and so on.

II
What is a Love Affair?

I n Part I of this exploration, we looked at the single
most important element in the difficult situation you
find yourself in – you: your feeling, thinking, experiencing Self. There were exercises in Part I to help you to
know yourself better, and also to develop a part of yourself that you may not have been aware of: your Observing
Self. There were also guidelines on how to use this part
of you to grow stronger and begin to re-integrate your
fragmented pieces into wholeness again. This may have
seemed too generalized and perhaps even too vague to be
truly useful in the everyday, concrete eventfulness of life,
but it was not intended to be a "cookbook" for each circumstance. It was intended as the beginning of an orientation, a framework, a perspective on your life. As we
progress through the parts of this process, specifics will
become clearer and more individualized as you relate
them to your unique situation. In this second section,

you are going to expand your perspective to include not just yourself, but your actual situation – your love affair with a married person. We will look very carefully at this relationship, searching for clues as to why this of all things can make you feel so bad at the same time that you feel so good.

This second part of the series is about facing truth and recognizing illusion in your love affair.

Correct Naming

The great Chinese philosopher Confucius said in the 5th century before Christ that "...*if terms be not correct, language is not in accordance with the truth of things ... therefore a superior man considers it necessary that the names he uses be spoken appropriately, and also that what he speaks may be carried out appropriately.*" *

In other words, names have power to influence how we see things and how we act, so it is important to make sure that important things are named as rightly as possible. Therefore, in order to get at the correct understanding of the structure and dynamics of any particular relationship, it is necessary first of all to be able to name it correctly, and also to name the roles people occupy within those relationships. This may seem obvious and even trivial, but it becomes important when we look deeply into the structure and dynamics of an affair.

---

* *The Analects of Confucius* XIII, 3, tr. Arthur Waley (NY: Vintage Books, 1989).

Structure

The structure of a relationship depends largely on its roles – the roles that people play make it recognizable as a certain kind of a relationship and these roles influence the people in them to act in certain predictable ways and allow them to have certain expectations. For example, the structure or shape of a parenting relationship is given by the biological or adoptive role-connections between parents (or surrogates) and their children. Parents will care for, raise, and support their children until the children are old enough to take care of themselves. The name "parent" ("mother," "father") is an important part of the shape of this relationship, because the name carries certain obligations and expectations with it – the obligation to nurture and educate the child, the expectation of having the child's respect. Typically, both parents and children expect and owe *love, loyalty, continuity, and trust* to each other. In addition, and this is significant for our discussion, they also owe each other *public acknowledgement* of the relationship.

Other ordinary relationships also carry a balance of specific obligations and expectations, which are clearly defined and identifiable by the correct names of both the relationships and the roles within them: *marriage* – husband, wife, spouse, mate; *friendship* – friends; *"being in love "* – girl friend, boy friend, "significant other." (There seems not to be a serious name in English either for the ordinary relationship characterized by being in love or for the roles within that relationship; it is not clear why this is so. "Girl friend" and "boy friend" are evocative of junior high school and seem not exactly suitable for adults, while "being in love" and "lovers" are too general, since they do not serve to distinguish the important way in which the contexts of being in love can differ.) It is important to note that *all* of these relationships carry expectations and obligations of trust, loyalty, continuity, and public acknowledgement. Typically, they are not expected to be either temporary or secret.

When speaking about an affair, an initial thing to notice about it is that it seems to have *two* names, both clear enough in that they correctly mark the difference between it and an ordinary "being in love" relationship; however, each name has its own distinctive aura that it shares with the role names within it. "Love affair" is actually a very attractive name, evoking romance, passion, and deep connection, as do the "lovers" within it. It does not immediately declare itself, as does an "extramarital affair," which reflects the bald truth right away, that it is in some way illicit. Accordingly, certain often-used names for the roles within an "extramarital affair" are loaded with pejorative connotations. What do we usually call the persons involved? Here are some unpleasant names you may have heard: cheat, mistress, philanderer, kept woman. Moreover, when the term "lover" is used in the same breath as "extramarital affair," it loses the attractive connotations it had within a "love affair" and often becomes an epithet that is meant to insult.

How can we account for this vast difference in connotation between two names for the same relationship? Perhaps it depends on what aspect of the relationship is uppermost in the mind of the namer. The lover of love may call it by one name; the lover of justice, another.

A major reason for marking the sense of injustice with bald labels and unpleasant names is because the relationship is, by definition, not public; it is secret, thus violating an important expectation in all other relationships. To love and to keep secret that love has powerfully damaging effects on the one who is loved; consider, for example, the difficult problems with self-esteem faced by so-called "illegitimate" children who are not publicly acknowledged by a parent, regardless of whether the parent makes an effort to contribute to the child's emotional and material well-being in other ways. An affair is secret because one of the partners is violating his or her obligations as a spouse and does not want this to be known. It is secret because outside the affair there would be tremendous disapproval of it and of the persons involved, due to the perceived violations of trust, loyalty, and marital obligations. The unpleasant names associated with the participants reflect the unease that is felt when fundamental moral obligations such as these are perceived to have been wilfully sidestepped. The unattached partner in particular is likely to have the additional burden of being seen as an intruder or predator, one who violates the sacred boundaries of someone else's marriage and family for the satisfaction of his or her own interests – a "homewrecker."

Under these circumstances, what obligations and expectations can the parties in such a relationship depend upon? The answers to this question suddenly bring the conflicted nature of love affairs to the surface. For example, one such set of expectations and obligations immediately involves the tangled issue of roles, because the unattached partner typically *expects to be a mate and to have a mate*. This becomes true very quickly regardless of what he or she "knows" about the other partner's being married – the drive for acknowledgement is strong and in the case of an affair goes directly against what is consciously "known." But the married partner already is a mate to someone else, and therefore wants only an occasional or part-time sexual and emotional friend, and perhaps even feels annoyed that the rules that were apparently agreed to have suddenly changed. On the other hand, the married partner typically wants the unattached partner to feel the *obligations* of a mate, for example sexual fidelity and emotional exclusivity, but at the same time he or she wants not to have to fulfill the *expectations* of a mate, namely sexual fidelity and exclusivity in return.

The most conflicted, perhaps even impacted, issue is that of secrecy. The very secrecy that makes the affair possible is experienced as humiliating and disparaging, regardless of the genuineness of the affection between the two lovers. The unattached partner wants – indeed, *needs* – openness and acknowledgement of the relationship; the married partner naturally wants to keep it largely or entirely secret and hidden. One partner naturally wants spontaneity and full access to the other, while the other requires rigidly careful planning and severely restricted access.

It is easy to see that in an affair, the roles of the partners are not "in sync" with each other; in fact they are largely in direct conflict.

Dynamics

The dynamic elements of a person are the psychological and emotional motivations that drive the individual to behave and act in uniquely varied ways – one's personality. This is part of what individuates and distinguishes each individual person from every other person.

Specific structural roles are the same in every kind of relationship, but we bring our individual dynamics – our personalities – into all of our relationship roles. For example, a mother is a mother wherever you look, but no two mothers are alike; each brings her unique individuality into her role.

This also makes all *relationships* different, because the parties to any relationship bring their own personalities into their roles, and the mix that results is an individualized blend or clash of these personalities and dynamics. Over time, each relationship then develops its own main dynamic – that combination of psychological and emotional elements that is most characteristic of it.

Specific roles within relationships also imply certain dynamics, but for our purposes we need to focus on only one: love or affection. All of the ordinary relationships above, as well as the uncommon love relationship we are most interested in here, have as a common role dynamic the self-evident obligation and expectation of love or affection. This also dictates that the main dynamic characteristic of all these *relationships* is also love and affection. People in their various roles feel the obligation to love the others in the relationship, and have the expectation that the others will love them back. There is a great human desire, even need, for love, and these expectations are so strong that if love is not present it is seen as a great and important problem that can and does hurt the integrity and strength of the relationship.

In a love affair, love is certainly there, very strongly, and often it is the only thing that really justifies the relationship and keeps it afloat. However, a second dynamic is also almost immediately present. In this sort of relationship, deep love can be side-by-side with deep anger and frustration almost right away precisely because of the conflicting expectations, desires, and obligations of the partners. Love affairs are the only relationships where frustration and anger are actually *built in* as a dynamic part of the relationship. Certainly, this does not mean that there is no anger and frustration in other relationships. The difference is that in other relationships, anger and frustration usually develop over time as a function of the interaction of the personalities involved, and any structural relationship imbalances also develop over time. In a love affair, the personalities of the partners may be extremely compatible and easy, but anger and frustration typically develop quickly and independently because of the immediately evident unbalanced nature of the role-connections.

To say that this is always true would be extreme—there are extramarital relationships which are well-balanced in this regard, either due to *both* parties' being married or due to the unattached partner's genuinely not wishing for more than is offered, choosing voluntarily to have an affair as an ideal arrangement that allows for maximum personal freedom while still enjoying a deep and passionate attachment. Remember that I am speaking specifically about the affair that is experienced as unbalanced: one married partner and one unattached partner, where this partner does not see the particular arrangement as desirable, fulfilling, or convenient.

A further cause of intense discomfort in the affair is the problem of the shadowy "third person" in the relationship – your lover's spouse. While you and your lover may or may not discuss this particular aspect of the issue openly, the knowledge is always there that your wonderful love is built almost completely on a web of lies and deceit by your partner, in which you have arguably played at least a passively cooperative role. Although it is not you who is being deceived and lied to, and it is not you who is actively deceiving and lying to the spouse, this issue eventually may have an insidious influence on the loyalty and trust within your affair.

Considering all the above, we might place a preliminary structural and dynamic description of a love affair between a married and a single person in something like these terms: it is a socially illicit, secret relationship, justified by the partners on its own terms, which are typically intense love and deep passion; but it is structured by mutually conflicting role elements which usually lead immediately to frustration and deep anger because these elements blur the clarity of expectations and obligations that are characteristic of ordinary relationships. This builds deep confusion and even emotional incoherence into the relationship right from the very beginning.

Furthermore, and this is significant, this profound confusion and lack of clarity is experienced simultaneously with strong structural imbalances that are skewed favorably toward one party in the affair, and unfavorably toward the other. Consider what people give and get in ordinary relationships. We mentioned some of these things briefly before – for example, a parent gives care and love to a child, a child in turn gives respect and affection to the parent. The give-get ratio is pretty well balanced by the nature of things; if it gets unbalanced, by a neglectful parent or a greedy child, there is a problem in the relationship which people feel deeply and which, because they feel it deeply, they might then try to work out.

In a love affair, giving and getting are unbalanced from the very beginning. What each partner wants to give is either not enough or too much for the other, and what each wants to get is more than or less than what the other wants to give. You may want to give me all your time and all your attention, but I only want to get it for a few hours a week. You may desire to get sexual fidelity from me, but I am married and can't give you what you want. Unbalanced expectations, desires, and obligations are probably present in all relationships to a degree, simply by the nature of the differences in individuals and their histories. In love affairs, however, these imbalances actually *define* the structure of the relationship to an unprecedented degree.

Meanwhile, the imbalances are not "symmetrical," so to speak. Unlike in an ordinary relationship, the partners in an affair are not on an equal or appropriately proportional footing where each partner can agree to give up something desired and a compromise is theoretically possible. The structure of ordinary relationships, even between parents and small children, make such negotiations and adjustments possible, sometimes even necessary.

For example, if a small child becomes ill and requires continuing round-the-clock attention for several days, a parent can, in principle, clear his or her time to provide the caretaking needed. Both parent and child are on an equal footing, in that the need to care for a small sick child is universally recognized as a mandate of parenthood and the parent need not invent lies in order to provide the care. The relationship is public. (I do not address here the issue of workplace policies, which may be in fact more or less sensitive to these issues. The point is that this analysis is true in principle.) In affairs, on the other hand, the imbalances are not even theoretically negotiable – the demand of secrecy ensures this and effectively "freezes" the status of each partner in place. As a result, the married partner in a love affair is usually pushing away excess, while the unattached partner is usually in a state of deprivation.

Notice that there is a big difference between having too much to eat, with the choice of leaving some of it behind, and not having enough to eat, with no choice to get more. This is the first important thing to notice about this unbalanced relationship; it is not only *unbalanced*, it seems also to be unfair.

Maintaining the Affair

Maintaining the affair then requires the unattached partner to *live with deprivation* as an essential part of continuing the relationship. It requires tremendous self-discipline to do that and eventually, in order not to feel frustrated all the time, the deprived partner must try to "outsmart" deprivation by learning actually to *want less*.

This is very difficult when deep emotion or desire are involved, if not impossible – try it when you are hungry.

Listen to what Epictetus, a 1st-century AD Stoic philosopher (who was born a slave) said: *"Demand not that events happen as you wish, but wish them to happen as they do happen, and you will get on well."** Can you do that? More importantly, should you expect yourself to?

The married partner, on the other hand, typically has an "embarrassment of riches" and essentially has a great deal more of what he or she wants – the filling of a vacant position ("lover") in the corporate structure of his or her life, without actually having to sacrifice anything crucial. This does not mean that the married partner does not love the unattached partner – it is simply a structural reality of his or her life. This is true even when the affair is accidental or unplanned – it *becomes* true when the decision is made to remain married. All the married partner ever has to do is manage the excess, the "leftovers."

Constantly having leftovers in the refrigerator is an inconvenience because one always has to figure out how to dispose of them. Usually they end up being thrown away – the food is wasted. Having an empty refrigerator or one with not enough food in it, on the other hand, is more than an inconvenience; it is a deprivation and can actually be dangerous to one's health if it is too empty too often.

---

* Epictetus, *Moral Discourses*, tr. Elizabeth Carter (London: J.M. Dent & Sons, Ltd., 1957), p. 258 (*Enchiridion* VIII).

Powerlessness

A major problem uncovered by these reflections is that it is the married partner who is apparently in control, in charge, typically because of the intricate schedule that must be maintained. The married partner has a whole other life that does not include his or her lover, and the appearance of the integrity of that married or domestic life has to be sustained at all costs. This means that your emotional life is probably on a rigidly fixed schedule – already unusual – and the schedule ends up depending on your married lover's availability (which may in turn depend upon your lover's *spouse's* plans). This can lead the unattached partner to feel not only humiliated and somewhat degraded, but eventually pretty powerless overall, and this is what may ultimately end up defining the dynamics of the relationship.

Typically, feeling powerless can express itself in several different ways. Sometimes, powerlessness in an unfair and seemingly unchangeable situation leads to feelings of *resignation, despair, depression, stagnation, and inertia* – a kind of "who cares" fatalism that is very unhealthy and can even rob one of the will to live, in extreme cases. At other times, it can lead to something the philosopher Friedrich Nietzsche called the "slave" mentality – feeling powerless can lead to *resentment, hostility,* and eventually to *passive-aggressive acts*, for example enslaving one's married partner in turn through guilt or threats of exposure. This is also very unhealthy, because it perverts one's natural spirit and turns love into something ugly.

A more desirable but less common outcome is the dawning recognition that the intense self-discipline of

managing scarcity that is required to remain in this relationship is an unfair burden. This recognition can lead to
anger, even to *rage*, and eventually to *revolt*. This is a
healthy outcome, because there is a growing understanding that one is simply worth more and deserves more
than what is being offered. It is only upon such recognition that one can begin planning to make rational
changes within the possibilities of the situation.

But it may seem that this analysis of a love affair is
unfair and unbalanced itself. Did we not agree that people
voluntarily make their own choices and are ultimately
responsible for them? How can we say it is "unfair" if it
was freely chosen? A good question. It is time to consider some moral issues – not "moralistic" ones, but things
like justice and fairness; duties, claims, and obligations;
integrity and self-respect.

Justice and Fairness

When we speak about justice and fairness in this context, it is important to be aware that we can speak of our
actions being just and/or fair, and we can also speak of our
relationships as being structured justly and/or fairly. I will
note here once again that I am not speaking of ill-inten-
tioned relationships based on some sort of self-interested
exploitation of one party by another; I am speaking
about two persons having fallen in love and making a
good-faith effort to honor that love in spite of emotionally and ethically difficult circumstances.

Beginning with actions, we can say that there is justice
in beginning a love affair, based on the idea of the free

agreement – an agreement voluntarily entered into by consenting adult persons of sound mind. Remember that I am assuming that we are not speaking of any kind of entrapment or seduction, but of a free choice. So the initial agreement must have been in some sense *just*. In the process of agreeing, both parties also presumably know what they are getting into – they know the "fundamental terms of their association," as the American philosopher John Rawls puts it. Specifically, the unattached partner knows that the other partner is married and is not going to change his or her status; each knows the situation of the other and accepts those facts. This means that the initial agreement must also have been in some sense *fair*.

The actual relationship, however, has a structure that seems to be independent of the voluntary actions and conscious knowledge of the participants in it. In the case of a love affair, the relationship itself seems intrinsically *unfair*, because it is explicitly structured to favor the needs of one of the partners over the needs of the other. It also seems *unjust* because the structure demands that one partner always have excess and the other always be deprived. (Remember here once again that I am explicitly speaking about an affair in which the imbalances are experienced as uncomfortable, and not of other situations where the arrangements may be perfectly suitable for both parties.)

After these reflections, we can tentatively say that the *agreement* between the lovers seems both fair and just, but that the *relationship they agree to* seems deeply unfair and also unjust. You can compare this to voluntarily agreeing to work in a job that requires a lot of very complex, heavy,

and difficult work for a salary of a dollar a day. Maybe
initially the job sounded so stimulating and interesting
that you might have been willing to work it for only a
dollar a day, but after a while, seeing that you are the
only one working so hard and getting so little, the
issues of fairness and justice become more compelling
than the interesting nature of the work – you either
want to be paid well for your work, or find another job.
This brings us to consideration of the obligations of an
unattached partner in a love affair with a married person – if you are the unattached partner, do you have a
right to ask for more "money" or to "find another job"?
Does your initially fair and just agreement bind you to
an unfair and unjust relationship on the original terms
of the agreement?

(The talk of "agreements" here may seem dry to the
point of dessication and far more suitable for discussions of contract law than passionate love. Clearly,
lovers do not formally sit down across a table with
lawyers in order to draft a formal agreement to have an
affair. Most of the agreements made by lovers are made
with the language of the eyes, with the play of gestures,
touch, and smell, and with a good deal of intuitive and
unspoken communication. I have deliberately left out
the delightful magic and the intriguing mystery of how
these agreements are actually made. Magic and mystery
can speak for themselves in love affairs, and usually do,
much more loudly than reason. Here, it is important to
let reason speak its piece, so I will let it do so without
being distracted by the sensual and emotional delights
of love affairs.)

Duties, Claims, and Obligations

Does your lover have any claims on you just because you love each other? How far does the initial agreement go? In other words, are there "rules" for love which say that once there is love in any context, there is a proper expectation of continuity, no matter what?

It seems to work that way in other situations. Parents expect their relationships with their children to change, but not to end. Married people hope that their marriage will not end and they enter into marriage, ideally, with the expectation that it will not; in fact they swear to it ("...'till death us do part"). Intimate friends also expect to be friends forever, or at least for a long time. All these relationships are based in love and affection, but love and affection in these cases incorporate something else as well, something vitally important to the relationship – action.

We spoke earlier of giving and getting. The things that we do for the people we love, and the things they do for us, require action – *doing*. Within all ordinary relationships, people can depend on certain actions from the people they love and they feel obligated to do certain things themselves. They may not experience these things as obligations, because they want to do them, but the obligations are built into the role whether they want to do them or not.

Ralph Waldo Emerson once spoke about the "citizenship" of love and friendship – the fact that it is expected that people who love each other and are friends do not love by words and feelings alone, they also must love by action: a husband sitting up with a sick wife; a mother rocking her colicky baby to sleep; friends lending each other money. Here is what he actually said; he is worth quoting:

> I do not wish to treat friendships daintily, but with roughest courage. When they are real, they are not glass threads or frostwork, but the solidest thing we know. ... I wish that friendship should have feet, as well as eyes and eloquence. It must plant itself on the ground, before it vaults over the moon. I wish it to be a little of a citizen, before it is quite a cherub. We chide the citizen because he makes love a commodity. It is an exchange of gifts, of useful loans; it is good neighborhood; it watches with the sick; it holds the pall at the funeral; and quite loses sight of the delicacies and nobility of the relation. ... We cannot forgive the poet if he spins his thread too fine and does not substantiate his romance by the municipal virtues of justice, punctuality, fidelity, and pity.[*]

This is the other side of romance – the "municipal virtues" that actually bind people together in the strong bonds of love. These actions typically balance themselves out over time; for example, the wife fixes her husband's favorite meal, the friend repays the loan on time, fifteen years later the colicky baby cuts the grass or does the dishes. This is not ledger-keeping or payback; it is the natural and organic balance of "citizenship" in love relationships.

---

[*] From his essay "Friendship". In Pakaluk, *Other Selves*.

What kind of citizenship can the partners in a love affair provide for each other, and once again, is it balanced or fair? When you have had a rough day, who is the person you most want to talk to about it? Can you call your married lover and talk it out? Probably not, since your lover is at home and not available by phone – at least not to you. On the other hand, if your lover has had a rough day, chances are he or she will find a way to call you and tell you all about it. When you are sick in bed with the flu for three days, will your married lover stay up with you and bring you hot tea and aspirin? Again, probably not, because you may only get a few hours a week and your illness may not coincide with the time available. Simple daily companionship through thick and thin, an ordinary characteristic of friendship and certainly one of Emerson's municipal virtues, is largely missing from love affairs. What do you do in the long, lovely summer evenings that you would have liked to share with your lover? On the other hand, does your lover's fixed schedule regularly conflict with your work time or other plans, and do you feel obligated to "make room"?

You can come up with your own scenarios of the citizenship of love, but ask yourself honestly: does the citizenship balance out? Are you getting, as they say, enough "action"? Or are you largely alone in providing citizenship responsibilities on demand, in step with a prescribed schedule that you have little or no control over? Even in ordinary relationships, once it becomes clear that the burdens of citizenship are unbalanced and are going to stay that way, there develops a sense of estrangement. Grown lazy kids get thrown out, husbands and wives separate, friends end their friendship. People feel taken advantage of if they appear to have most of the burdens of citizenship, while the parties to a relationship who regularly provide less citizenship feel compelled to justify and rationalize their lack of participation.

So it seems that even in ordinary relationships, balance of action is important for the continuation of the relationship. It is also true in an uncommon love relationship that balance is necessary, or there is a risk that it will not last; this may be the source of the common wisdom that "affairs always end." The key to the problem of whether there are claims on you to remain in the love affair is to remember that the original agreement between you and your lover was brought about mostly because of the love and affection that you felt for one another. But the problem is this: if action or citizenship is an important, even necessary, part of love and affection, and it is obvious that you are and will continue to be regularly short-changed in this department, you need to ask yourself whether any love relationship that distributes its burdens and benefits so unevenly can properly obligate you to stay in it. Is the agreement itself not void on its own terms?

Integrity and Self-Respect

There are more subtle questions here which are very important because they tap into romantic mythologies that many of us share. Many people believe that all loving relationships have "integrity" regardless of their contexts. This is a romantic point of view which says, in effect, that love conquers all. So an important question becomes whether love *should* really "conquer all," including the kinds of harms and hurts that love affairs bring. In other words, are there things in life more important than love, or at least equally important?

One way to approach the answers to these questions is to reflect on what we just discussed – the citizenship of love. We said that in love affairs there was much love, passion, and other intense emotion, but by the nature of things, very little balance of citizenship or action. What is also true is that unless yours is one of the very rare cases, your married lover will not take any independent action to end his or her marriage and begin a new life with you. The status quo will continue until and unless you change it.

What are the implications of this? Very simply, that the deepest, most intense, most powerful and enduring feelings you possibly have ever had, seem to make absolutely no difference to the way things are – they are, in effect, apparently irrelevant. How can that be?

We are used to having powerful feelings that are very naturally followed by some sort of action based on those feelings. But in a love affair, your powerful feelings of love, your intense passion, and your deep devotion are followed by very little action or sometimes no action at all, again due to the built-in structural restraints of the kind of relationship this is. The effects of what you feel so deeply are therefore confined only to the actual encounters with your lover that you have – in other words, all your encounters are completely self-contained and compartmentalized.

What "effects" are we speaking of here? The author

Michael Drury calls this unusual situation "loving in real time." * All there is, she says, is your love, your meetings, your conversations, your lovemaking. There is no active, open carry-over into the rest of your lives as there would be in an ordinary love relationship between single people, where powerful feelings of love, passion, and devotion would naturally lead to public, mutual, active commitments and life changes of various sorts. When we speak about the integrity of love, it is precisely these "external" commitments that we are speaking of, and not just the deep internal emotions and passions of love.

In uncommon love relationships such as this one, your lives are likely to continue on as before, to the outside observer largely unchanged and unaffected by the powerful emotions and expectations your affair has generated. No matter how much your married partner loves you or how deeply you feel about it, he or she will not be there to bring you tea when you are sick and will not ever change your status as a married person's lover. Furthermore, not only does it not matter how much you love, it also doesn't matter how much you hurt, or whether you reveal to your partner how much you love or hurt. None of it will ever make any *actual* difference, even though your lover may be genuinely gratified by your love and genuinely remorseful for your hurt.

It may be the core of self-respect to believe as a matter of course that one's life and all that one feels and thinks are, on some level, deeply important – that they *matter*. If you do believe that, how does it feel to think of

---

* Michael Drury, *Advice to a Young Wife From an Old Mistress* (NY: Random House, 1995).

your deep and powerful feelings as ultimately irrelevant? It is the answer to this question that will begin to address the issue of whether love should conquer all. How much of your humanity and self-respect must you give up to agree voluntarily that your deep and powerful feelings don't really need to matter?

At this point, it might be worthwhile to note another Latin root, this time for the word "action." The root is from "agere," *to do*. Notice the related concepts of action, being active, and being an agent (or one who acts); compare these with the opposing concepts of passion, being passive, being (a) patient. In the first set of terms, we get the feeling of movement, power, taking initiative, doing things; in the second set, there is a feeling of being swept away by something or someone, letting things happen, being powerless, or enduring things that are done around or to you.

It is this contrast between action and passion that needs to be looked at very carefully, because it is only by changing your own status in your love affair from passive to active that you have a chance of changing some of the imbalances, restoring some of the integrity of love, and re-establishing self-respect.[*]

---

[*] It is important to remember here that these explorations of love affairs are not concerned with judging their overall morality. We are not looking for an answer to the question, "Is it morally permissible to have love affairs?" We are accepting the fact that we do have love affairs, whether they are "permissible" or not. The larger issues of integrity and self-respect, seen from that perspective, are therefore not our concern here; the more local issues, *within the existing relationship*, are.

Beginning the Change

We have spent a lot of time talking about how the structures of these relationships can damage or harm the people in them if they are not careful and aware, and why that is so. Now it is time to talk about how to start the process of change so you are clear enough and strong enough to make informed decisions about the nature of your participation in your affair. In all cases, it is going to be your strong, active, and aware self that will act, not your weak, passive self that will react.

We spoke earlier about your Observing Self, an essential part of you that can be taught to be independent of your emotional and psychological experience. If you remember, your Observing Self can stand "outside" you and observe you going through your life in a dispassionate sort of way. It can inform you objectively of what the person who is you is doing, feeling, and thinking, providing a calm and neutral counterpoint to your own emotionally charged lived experience. It is something like the point of view you have when you watch your own self doing things in a dream.

You may think you don't really need to be "informed" – after all, you are the one going through all this. But the "experiencing" part of you is likely to be caught up in confusion and emotion and unable, perhaps even unwilling, to assess your situation accurately; it is the dispassionate and unsentimental part of you that can help to focus things into their proper perspective. It will do so simply by standing aside and describing to you what you are doing. The key is that this Observer is clear-eyed and unemotional and not wrapped up in the confusion and suffering of your experiencing self.

Are you feeling ready to face things as they actually are, and not just through a romantic haze of passion and suffering? Here are three "truth-and-illusion" exercises for gaining a more accurate perspective on your love affair. Once again, these are written exercises, and depend for their effectiveness on your taking the time to do them carefully and seriously.

Exercise 5

The Cave

Plato has a wonderful story about coming out of the dark cave of illusion, where only the shadows on the wall seem real, into the bright light of the sun, which can initially blind you but later lets you see reality clearly.[*] At that point, you can see the difference between truth and illusion and recognize that you have been in a cave.

The confusion and suffering that you have been going through is partially due to your being lost in a "cave" – your feelings and ideas about your love affair. This is perfectly understandable, since we saw exactly how the emotions, passions, structure, and dynamics of this kind of relationship can cause you to lose your way. But perhaps what you want

---

[*] You can find this story in "Republic VII," in *Plato: The Collected Dialogues*, eds. Edith Hamilton and Huntington Cairns (Princeton, NJ: Princeton University Press, 1989).

now is to come out of the cave and into the bright sunlight, to see your cave for what it actually is.

The first thing is to describe the cave from inside, before you have made the first steps to come out of it.

▪ What is your cave, your love affair, really like? Describe what your love affair looks like and feels like **from inside**. Talk about what you think and what you feel when you are waiting for your lover to contact you, when you and your lover are finally together, when your lover leaves to return to his or her other life. Talk about how it feels to talk to your lover, to make love with him or her. Talk about the intimacy and friendship of your time together. Talk about the loneliness, anger, and sadness of your time apart. Talk about any bewilderment or confusion you feel when you do not understand why things are the way they are.

▪ Use other **concrete details** from your love affair in your description. How do you dress for your lover? Has your physical appearance changed since you began your affair? Do you have any outside activities that you and your lover enjoy together? Movies, music, poetry readings, bowling? Or is your time mostly spent secluded away from the public eye? How do you feel when you are out with your lover and people see you? Are you happy, proud, uncomfortable, uneasy? How do you feel if you are usually secluded? Comfortable, resentful, restless, secure?

Comments:

Take some time with this exercise. It is an emotionally difficult one and you may find it helpful to think about it for a while before you write anything down. Again, use vivid, descriptive words, and don't be surprised at what you find yourself writing about your cave. Overall, is it dark and confining? Is it warm and cozy? Both? Is the "sunlight" outside a bit threatening? Do you feel safe inside the cave, even though it is sometimes cold and lonely? Do you actually *want* to lose any of your illusions? Be very, very honest with yourself here, and remember, no one is going to know what you write unless you give your permission, so try not to edit yourself.

Exercise 6

Letter from the Observer

This time, allow your Observing Self to go out of the cave and take up a position in the sunlight where it can see the cave clearly. This vantage point allows the Observer to see the shape of the cave from outside, but also allows a clear view into the inside of the cave.

- Have your Observing Self write you a letter describing the view, unemotionally. What does your cave actually look like to the dispassionate Observer, both inside and outside? Is the darkness inside murky and atmospheric, or is it soft and welcoming? Is the sunlight warm and brilliant, or is it harsh and unforgiving?

- How does your Observer see your affair? Where you experience intimacy, friendship, loneliness, and resentment, for instance, what does your Observer see? How do your activities with your lover appear to the objective eye?

- How does your Observer see you? From the dispassionate point of view, do you appear strong? Weak? Confused? Clear? Does your Observer see you creating some of your own illusions, or wall-shadows? What kind of illusions? For example, are you a story-teller? Do you make up stories to force your situation to make some sense? An example of a common story is, "We are just dear friends who happen to sleep together, so none of this really applies to me." What stories does your Observer hear you inventing?

Comments:

Again, this requires some thought, and, let's face it, some courage, and again, you may want to take some time to think about this carefully before you actually have your Observer write the letter. Remember to be completely honest and also, remember not to allow your Observing Self to be caught up in your emotions and confused thoughts. Be clear, dispassionate, unemotional – as if you were talking about and describing someone else.

Exercise 7

Making Your Case

Now that you've "received a letter" from your Observing Self, do you find yourself feeling a little defensive? In other words, do you feel like you want to argue with the clear-eyed observations of you and your situation that you "read" in the letter? Go ahead! This third exercise asks you to do exactly that: make your case.

▪ Write down all the good reasons – love, passion, excitement, intimacy, friendship – why your love affair is important enough and special enough to swallow some of the injuries and indignities that your Observer saw and described to you in the letter; make the case that love really does conquer all. (By the way, **did** your Observer see any indignities and injuries? If not, what, do you make of that?)

▪ If you really want to have an interesting and productive experience of self-exploration with this exercise, write it in the form of a dialogue or play between you and your Observer, and argue both sides of the case as strongly as possible.

In this set of exercises, your perspective will definitely be split into two competing views. This will loosen you up somewhat, as you go back and forth between your experiencing self and your Observing Self – passionate against dispassionate, involved against uninvolved, attached against detached. Remember to make the best case possible for each side.

Comments: Self-protection and Illusion

You have just completed three very intense exercises which have taken a good deal of strength and courage (or should have, if you have done them seriously). Again, as with the last series of exercises in Part I, ask yourself how you feel. What is your major feeling tone? Do you feel calm, anxious, relieved, happy, upset, angry, sad? Give the exact names of the feelings you have – remember what Confucius said: that it is important to name important things correctly so you can choose correct actions. If you are not sure of your feelings, describe your confusion; in other words, describe in what way your feelings aren't clear. For example, are you conflicted between relief and resentment? Do you feel as though you just want to run away from thinking about this whole thing? Be specific.

If you feel generally good, ask yourself whether you have been honest about your feelings or whether you have been protecting yourself by putting the best face on them. Again, as with our previous discussion of "denial," this is for you to decide – no one except your Observing Self can tell you the truth about your feelings; even so, you must open yourself to the possibility of truth; you must allow it to happen.

Then, ask yourself whether what you think about your love affair has changed since starting this set of exercises. In the dialogue with your Observer, where each of you made the best case possible, who "won"? Whose case was better? What were the highlights of that case? If it turned out that your case (the case from "inside" your affair) was better, what do you think of that? Do you think it is an honest assessment, or are you allowing your illusions to have more weight than the truth?

What is wrong, one might ask, with having illusions or protecting oneself? The answer is, absolutely nothing. Everyone is entitled to have defenses and protections – there is no law that says that everyone must face the harsh reality of their lives at all times. If illusions are helpful and smooth your path while you are gathering your strength, that's fine. The only thing that would be even more helpful is for you to recognize them as illusions while consciously allowing yourself to "believe" in them for a while longer. If you are feeling too vulnerable right now to allow your real feelings to be fully present to you, it is perfectly

fine to protect yourself against them for a while longer –
to push them away, down below the surface of consciousness. Again, however, it is valuable to acknowledge to
yourself that that is what you are doing, if you can.

Why do we need to protect ourselves with illusions?
Doesn't that mean that we are not mature, or something
like that? The truth is that we often tell ourselves stories
that seem kinder than the brute facts of our lives. This is
the way we survive from day to day while we slowly work
to get strong enough to confront our truths. What many
people recognize about facing truth is that at the same
time we give up our illusions we also give up whatever
hope we had in the particular area that our illusions support. Truth is often harsh and is illuminated with a bright
and clear light – the "sunlight" outside the cave; outlines
and textures become clearly visible and there is nowhere
to hide. It is very hard to think about giving up hope, even
if we realize in the light of truth that what we had was false
hope.

Another thing most people recognize, usually on a more
unconscious level, is that once we face the truth, we usually feel we have to do something about it – to act – and
action usually means change. Most people are very naturally hesitant about change – remember the saying,
"Better the devil you know than the devil you don't
know"? This series of explorations and exercises have as
their specific purpose a program to help you face the possibility of change, and their point of view is that change
does not have to be for the worse or something to be
feared. Moreover, this program is not furthering an ideo-
logical or moralistic agenda to get you to change something in particular, such as leaving your relationship

whether you want to or not. Although you may actually decide to do just that, the point is that it will be *your* decision, not anyone else's. In fact, by strengthening yourself and facing your truths, you will have the means at hand to decide *not* to change your basic situation – you may very well decide to continue your affair, but there might be some differences in your perspective and in how you feel.

One difference will be that this time remaining in your relationship will be your conscious and reflective decision, made with full knowledge, from a position of inner strength, as opposed to something that "happens" to you that you feel you have no control over (remember "passion" and being "passive"?). Another difference is that you will also know how to change certain things within your relationship so that it is balanced more evenly and does not injure you as much as it has in the past. Part IV of this series will show you concrete and practical ways to do just that.

For now, your struggle is with truth itself. How much of your truth do you feel you want to know? How much of it can you handle at once? Maybe you feel you need more time to ease yourself into facing it, one step at a time. Remember, you are in charge of this process. There is no one standing around with a stop watch telling you that you must meet some sort of a deadline. There is no one telling you that you actually have to do any of this at all. You may not be ready to give up your illusions just yet, and that is perfectly fine – the events of our lives often have their own imperatives and time tables that need to be respected. What these reflections offer you is a program for when you are ready. And you will find that once you have gathered your courage to face your truths and face down your false hopes and illusions, you will be able to change things for the better, one way or another, and you will be in control of your life once again.

In this second part of the series you have courageously looked at some of the darker truths about your love affair that you may have preferred not to look at before, because you were wrapped up in love, intimacy, and passion and were afraid to lose those very important things. You now know, or will soon realize, that you can face the truth and not have to lose them if you don't wish to.

III
Having Sex, Making Love

s must be obvious by now, the single partner in a love affair with a married person typically undergoes a great deal of suffering as reality sets in and begins to co-exist with the feelings of intense love and passion that are characteristic of such a relationship. In the two previous sections, we looked at how the inherently unbalanced structure of such a love affair works to foster a fragmentation of the Self. This then increases the suffering by adding feelings of powerlessness to the mix of intense emotions, both positive and negative, which the unattached partner is already experiencing. Feeling powerless may then foster a kind of passivity which serves to maintain the status quo and gradually increases the confusion and suffering of the unattached partner. In this section, we will begin to look at how it might be possible to re-awaken the active part of the Self and use it to begin re-integrating into wholeness. After that, we can explore how this newly integrated self can actively begin to change the imbalances in the relationship to make it more fair and equitable.

We will begin to do this by exploring the nature of passion, eroticism, and sex, as well as the protocols and etiquette of love, friendship, and intimacy in a love affair.

Previously, we linked passion and passivity linguistically because of their common Latin root, "pati" or "patior," which means *to suffer, to experience, to endure, or to submit to*. This was to show how easily and naturally passion, which is desirable in a love affair, can lead to passivity, which is not desirable. In this section, we are going to try to separate them, so that you can throw out the bathwater without also throwing out the baby – so you can be passionate and have passion in your love affair without letting it drag you down into passivity, leaving you vulnerable to injury.

"Surrender"

Many people recognize that passionate love cannot exist unless there is some sort of surrender on the part of both partners. Earlier we spoke about how passionate love reflects our ability and desire to let ourselves be "carried away" and to let go of control. Passionate love of this sort is so full of beauty and grace that we naturally want the experience to continue, to expand beyond lovemaking itself. Partially because of this, surrender to passion can easily lead to letting go of control in other areas as well, which can then further lead into passivity.

But there is a big difference between surrender to passion and surrender into passivity.

Surrender to passion is generative, creative, and empowering, and absolutely necessary for full erotic and emotional fulfillment in any love relationship, including an uncommon one such as this. *Generative* means that you can produce or originate something; *creative* means that this can be something new; and *empowering* means that your relationship strengthens your sense of self and your belief that you can be generative and creative. What exactly is it that we are "surrendering" when we experience passion in lovemaking? We are letting go, voluntarily and temporarily, of the judging, analyzing, evaluating part of ourselves – our *cognitive* capabilities – and giving our undivided *sensual* and *emotional* attention to the moment we are in and to the person we are with, unconditionally.

Surrender into passivity, on the other hand, drains you of your strength, favors inertia rather than creativity, and leads to stagnation rather than generation. *Draining* means literally that your strength and power are exhausted just by the effort of maintaining your connection to your relationship without losing too many essential parts of yourself; *inertia* means that you do not have the energy to move something away from the path it is already taking; and *stagnation* means that nothing new is being created or generated in your relationship.

Consider what happens in lovemaking. In an ideal erotic relationship, both partners can take turns being dominant, active, setting the pace, and allowing the other partner to "surrender," to relax into sensuality and emotion. When your partner allows you to surrender in this way he or she is in fact giving you a wonderful gift, the gift of safely allowing the world (your partner) to make the decisions for you for a brief and lovely time. Your act of surrender, in its turn, gives your partner the gift of trust. Your letting go of control in lovemaking is an expression of that love and trust, an invitation for him or her to cross boundaries that no one else is permitted to cross, to be in contact with you in a way that is essential and precious. It is a reflection of the value you place upon your partner as a person.

There then develops a very natural desire to surrender control in other areas as well, with the thought that this experience of beauty and grace can be carried over into other areas of the relationship as well. This desire is probably not even conscious, but more of an acquired way of being, reinforced by what you feel when you surrender in lovemaking. This, however, may not have the desired or expected effect. Even in an ordinary love relationship, where both partners are single and fully available to each other, a one-sided overall surrender of control usually leads to difficulties, because the relationship eventually becomes unbalanced. If one person is usually in control, and the other usually follows along, increasingly passively, a number of things can happen.

Resentments can grow on both sides for different reasons. The dominant or active partner may resent always having to be in charge; the passive partner may come to resent not being able to influence what happens. More importantly, there is little opportunity for the growth of the partners, either individually or together; the relationship quickly assumes a level of stagnation as the partners settle into their limited roles. This encasement then becomes a prison of security for both partners as a kind of comfort level with stagnation is reached, and typically such a relationship can go on for years, unfulfilling to anyone.

Another thing that may happen is that one partner can become *domineering* (rather than just dominant) and begin to enjoy the power that he or she has over the other person. Then the other partner can easily come to feel, or even actually to be, victimized. Usually, people do not allow this to go too far before recognizing that adjustments need to be made; if adjustments are not made, however, the relationship can gradually become pathological, perhaps even dangerous.

These are some pitfalls in ordinary relationships – perhaps you recognize them from your own life or from the lives of your friends and relatives. But in an uncommon love relationship, severe imbalances are already built in from the very beginning as basic structural and dynamic elements; in this circumstance, allowing yourself to let go of control in too many other areas of the relationship can lead to damage and injury to your inner, essential self almost immediately. This is one reason that anger is the other dominant dynamic in a love affair, next to love – because such loss of power *feels* almost unavoidable, due to the special circumstances of an affair, and on the other hand, there is a recognition that it does not need to *be* unavoidable, if only the married partner would "do the right thing."

But why would a person let go of control so easily in a love affair, as opposed to an ordinary love relationship?

Here is where the issue of "scheduling" assumes an even greater importance than before. Besides the natural desire to surrender control in order to extend the beauty and grace of lovemaking, just on a practical level it seems you almost *must* do so anyway because your married part-ner has a double life and cannot simply spontaneously decide on the spur of the moment to spend time with you. So scheduling your time together seems necessarily to be your partner's responsibility. This may seem rela-tively harmless on the face of it, but earlier we looked carefully at how damaging it eventually becomes to have your emotional life so severely rationed and scheduled in the first place, and especially to have it be your partner, and not you, who is always in charge of the timetable. Remember also that this timetable often depends on your partner's *spouse's* activities and plans, the "shadow third." This issue of scheduling, so matter-of-fact and seemingly innocuous on the surface because it is so practical, usual-ly acts insidiously to turn one of the partners passive and powerless and sets the stage for further relinquishing of control.

There is also a more subtle and frightening cause for the easy surrender into passivity. Your married partner has already shown you that he or she feels a great deal of freedom to cross strong, socially-reinforced boundaries of marital obligation and responsibility. This is not as easy to do as it sounds, and it is not quite as common-place as TV and films (and maybe your lover) would have you believe. It requires a very strong sense of self and a strong sense of entitlement to be able not only to give oneself permission to cross those boundaries but also to sustain, perhaps for years, the secret double life that follows. The subliminal message that this often sends is that this person is free enough to walk away from obligations to you also, if you do not do what is expected; that he or she may not ever be as "imprisoned" by your mutual love and passion as you are. Moreover, because of the illicit nature of the relationship, the issue of obligations between the partners is not clearly defined to begin with, as we have seen, and is therefore experienced as more tenuous and less reliably solid than in an ordinary relationship.

This may not actually be true – often your married partner is in fact as "captivated" by your love affair as you are. But the message that your partner is essentially free to walk away from you is deeply unconscious. Whatever evidence you may have to the contrary, such as your lover's sincere declarations of love or his or her regular presence in your life, the subliminal message does its work very well. The anxiety of losing your love affair works as a powerful motivation to keep you doing whatever you feel is necessary to keep it going, and too often this may lead to a passive cooperation in your own injury.

An even more subtle process often is at work here as well. The philosopher Simone de Beauvoir underlined the dangers of a complete surrender of autonomy by noting that giving the self completely was likely to be a "flight from freedom," an idea that is echoed by many Existential thinkers; the idea is that it is frightening for human beings to be free to choose, to act, and to take responsibility, so that surrender even to an unbalanced or harmful situation, where control (and choice) is given to someone else, relieves that anxiety and lends a feeling of security. In such a tenuous and unclear situation as a love affair, if the various surrenders of control occur early on, the habit of deferring to the partner becomes deeply set in and a matter of course very quickly; at that point, it can be perceived as doubly threatening and dangerous to disturb the delicate status quo by asserting one's own desires and needs. It is much more reassuring to have your partner make all the decisions. All you have to deal with then is your own hurt, anger and resentment, whereas on the other hand, too much rebellion might lead to a devastating loss – the loss of the affair altogether. As we have seen, this flight from freedom creates a false security and may be dangerous if carried to an extreme.

How is it possible for all these things to go on outside of awareness? The writer D.H. Lawrence once wrote a story indirectly offering support for the flight-from-freedom idea ("The Virgin and the Gypsy") which implied that passion cannot co-exist with reason and further, that one must be literally unconscious in order to surrender to passion. In his view, even the erotic relinquishing of control we spoke of earlier requires the permission granted by some sort of external natural disaster of some sort – it is a decision too fearful for one to make voluntarily on one's own. In his story it was, appropriately enough, a flood. According to this point of view, one needs to be overwhelmingly "flooded" with passion in order to surrender to it, and because one is flooded and unconscious, one may then also surrender one's reason and awareness. Significantly, it then becomes easier to become a victim in one's own eyes and to blame passion itself for the abrogation of one's own responsibilities as a free person choosing freely.

None of the above scenarios needs to apply to you. I

will show you how to eat your cake (surrender to passion, beauty, and grace) and have it, too (maintain your freedom to act by using your reason to participate fully in your affair as the co-writer, the co-author of the script).

Time

One of the ways you can begin to free yourself is by considering how time operates in your relationship. Time has practically everything to do with the issues we have been discussing. In the previous section, we spoke briefly about how your meetings and encounters with your lover must, by the nature of things, be compartmentalized and self-contained – that there can be no carry-over of what you experience with your lover into the rest of your life. This, as we saw, is radically different from what happens in an ordinary love relationship, where what you experience together is expected to carry over; plans are altered to accommodate the relationship, lives are changed, families and friends are brought into the circle of your happiness, and so on.

Typically, in a love affair with a married person, none of this can or does take place. Everything that there actually is between you takes place only when you are together. Anything else "carries over" only in your minds or in your hearts, not in your actual, lived lives – not in citizenship. We remarked that the author Michael Drury calls this "loving in real time." Even in a special circumstance such as an affair between co-workers, where there is often opportunity to alter the working environment in such a way as to increase the amount of work time spent together, it is still necessary to use the requirements of the job as an excuse and a cover; it is still not permissible to make the relationship open. (Many workplaces, of course, frown on romantic relationships between colleagues altogether, whether they are socially illicit or not.)

What this means, first of all, is that you will have serious psychological adjustments to make, that you will have to experience a shift in your normal attitudes toward time. St. Augustine had some interesting things to say about time. He remarked that " ... the past now has no existence and the future is not yet" and that furthermore "... the present is so made that it passes into the past [so] how can we say that this present also 'is'?"* He concluded that past, present, and future always co-exist somehow in our minds as our experience of time.

The psychologist Fritz Perls had a different approach, but ended up recognizing essentially the same thing as St. Augustine. He felt, however, that in our lived lives this confluence of past, present and future in our minds tends constantly to shape our ideas and actions around the past or toward the future, while the present moment goes by essentially unnoticed. This tends to sacrifice the importance and authenticity of the present, the actual lived moment. He recommended, therefore, that we as healthy people ought to practice living "here and now," taking full responsibility for what is here in front of us or within us, instead of constantly re-living the past or living in anticipation of the future.†

---

* Augustine, *Confessions* X. 17, 18, tr. Henry Chadwick (NY: Oxford University Press, 1992).

† Fritz Perls, e.g., *Gestalt Therapy Verbatim* (NY: Bantam Books, 1969), and other works.

These ideas are significant for us in our explorations of love affairs. In an uncommon love relationship, it turns out that we have to take seriously and literally the advice to live "here and now," and we have to be aware of how deeply influenced we are by our past (our memories and stereotypes) and our future (our expectations, based on those memories and stereotypes).

In an ordinary love relationship, as soon as we feel happiness and joy, we anticipate and expect that this is also the way it will be tomorrow and for the foreseeable future. This is because our memory (our past) tells us that this is how things are in the world; this continuity in a relationship is normal and to be expected. In an uncommon love relationship, this happens also, instinctively and unreflectively, regardless, as we have seen, of what is actually "known." This is because the heart is not sophisticated; all it ever knows how to do is to love and to grieve. It doesn't – can't – "think" about the realities of the situation. It knows that it loves, that it feels joy, and it knows that this ought to carry over into tomorrow and innocently expects that it will, and is crushed and bewildered when it doesn't.

It is the mind, our reason, that reminds our heart that this is not going to happen – that as soon as your meeting with your lover is over, it's over, until the next meeting. Until then, you live your life alone, as before. Your actual lived life has not changed to accommodate your love, and it won't. To your chagrin, your lover's life also remains as before, unchanged.

Notice that this is a major example of the fragmentation of the self that we discussed earlier. Your mind must constantly remind your heart that things aren't going to proceed in the normally expected way. Your heart, on the other hand, constantly and stubbornly insists that love has its own rules and that certainly things *will* happen in the expected way. You are at war with yourself. What can you do? The answer is that you can begin to learn to discipline yourself away from both your memory and your expectations, and pay a different kind of attention to the present, the lived here and now.

This will lead you to the other side of the coin of not being able to incorporate your lover into the rest of your life; loving a person in "real time" has certain characteristic pleasures and depths that typically are not easily available to other, more socially normalized loves. Consciousness of severely rationed time in a love affair often leads to a natural desire to make the most of the time available and can give each precious moment spent in each other's presence a crystal-clear agenda – to focus great attention upon each other and upon the love that is shared. Without social and domestic distractions, such as managing a household, arguments over money, attention to children's needs, or socializing with friends, each moment assumes freshness and depth. Even as lovers are discussing politics or watching television, their consciousness is always upon each other.

It is likely that because of this both lovers will be mindful of appearing in the best light to one another in the short time available, so personal appearance tends not to take on the cheerful carelessness of familiarity as quickly as in other arrangements. It is the same with conduct; lovers are on their "best" behavior more often and more easily because the distractions that arise from daily domestic familiarity typically do not appear in a love affair, and arguments about extraneous things tend to be carefully managed so as not to assume too much importance. With such concentrated attention and care for each other, sustained for years in some cases, lovers often find that their love and passion actually grow in scope, depth, and texture over time, because their love is the main focus of their attention while they are together regardless of whatever activity they happen to be engaged in.

It is interesting that this benefit appears to be almost unique to love affairs, because it is clear that it need not be. Marriages can certainly be focused on passionate love, and some have been, incorporating domesticity and familiarity without losing passion. Unfortunately, this seems to be the exception and not the rule. In a marriage or other relationship where the social and structural context is easily lived with and undemanding as such, and perhaps even *because* of this, love and passion typically tend quickly to fade into the background and stay there, with only brief reappearances now and then if ever. In a love affair, on the other hand, the situation is almost reversed. Because of the intense demands of attention and self-discipline required to sustain a love affair, there is little opportunity or desire to take love for granted; passionate love is nurtured as the central focus and purpose of the relationship and passionate togetherness clothes the lovers' contacts.

This, of course, may make it all the more difficult to contemplate ending the affair, since it is unlikely that passionate love will be sustained like this in alternative, meaning ordinary, relationships. In fact, "ordinary" is a tragically appropriate word that applies perfectly to too many marriages and other arrangements, as partners become caught up in the extraneous demands of everyday life and allow the love that brought them together to fade to the periphery of awareness. Once one has had the taste of the "extraordinary," however, one is usually not easily willing to give it up and to settle once again for the other.

This radical readjustment of your attitudes toward time may be uncomfortable at first, but eventually it has these and other very positive and beneficial effects. Learning to attend to the present moment is a powerful corrective for all sorts of problems people can have in the living of ordinary life; in the living of an unusual or uncommon life, such as you are doing, it becomes essential and ultimately deeply rewarding.

To be sure, this all may sound awfully vague – what does "attending to the present moment" or "living in the here and now" actually amount to in the real world? Here is a very simple way to focus yourself in the present, using sex and your memory and imagination.

Exercise 8

Having Sex, Making Love

This exercise might work better as a contemplative exercise rather than a written one, since writing may distract you.

- *Sit quietly and comfortably alone somewhere where*

you can relax completely and not be interrupted by anything or anyone. This exercise asks you to take yourself
through a lovemaking experience in your mind. You can use
your memory, if you like, to try to recall a particular time
when you and your lover made love, or you can use your
imagination to develop a lovemaking fantasy. (In this specific case, the use of memory and anticipation will foster the
quality of being in-the-moment that is the point of this exercise.) The important thing is to pay very close attention **now**
to what is going on in memory or imagination; step by step,
moment by moment, be there fully in the moment, in real
time. Do not let yourself be distracted by other thoughts,
such as your busy schedule for the week, or a problem you
may be having with your children, or anything else. This
would be an improper use of memory and anticipation, and
would take you out of the moment that you are trying to
create for yourself. Just indulge yourself, for as long or as
short a time as you like; do so with full attention and without distraction.

• Be fully aware of every caress, every sensation, every
anticipation that develops in your imaginary lovemaking.
"See" your lover's body, "feel" your lover's hands and lips,
"smell" the characteristic aromas of your lovemaking, "hear"
the sounds that you and your lover make, "taste" your lover's
sweetness. If you are doing this exercise with full attention,
you ought to experience some physiological changes as
your body prepares itself for actual lovemaking. When you
have finished this playful exercise without allowing any distractions, you will have some idea of what it means to be
here now, to live fully in the moment.

Comments:

The most important question is this: what is it like for
you when you are actually making love? Are you fully

aware of all these things, and only these things, while you are making love? If not, if your mind is a million miles away and working on something else, then you are not really making love – you are "having sex," sort of in the same way that you would "have" a pizza or a scotch-and-soda.

But when you are really making love, you are in the here and now, with no thought or feeling for anything else except what you are actually doing or experiencing, moment by moment. Notice also that in the here and now, your lover becomes an actual person in the lived present, one who is momentarily *not* the subject of any negative or romantic stereotypes. Your lover in the here and now is the person you love, the person on whose account you experience passion; he or she is not the person who is "causing" such distress and problems in your life.

This is the here-and-now mind-set which will allow you to develop your own realistic and strong boundaries, the subject of the next discussion. Your love affair can become an extremely effective laboratory for you to re-experience and strengthen your real, essential self, as you confront your tendency to allow your memories, expectations, resentments, and stereotypes to dictate your feelings, thoughts, and actions in the present moment.

This will occur in the following way. Reflect upon the discussion of relationships and roles in the previous section. Remember that we said that all ordinary relationships have recognizable roles within the relationship, all of which have specific identifying names – mother, husband, nephew, friend. Now, here you are in a relationship that has no recognizable roles and only pejorative or ambiguous identifiable names. Earlier, we saw that this was one of the factors that made an uncommon love relationship difficult to understand and that immediately set certain negative stereotypes into motion. Here, we can look at the other side of that coin as well. Now that you are beginning to develop a here-and-now orientation to your experience, the lack of clearly defined roles can actually help you to consider yourself free to create your own roles without playing out any pre-established scripts. Here you can see that you have an opportunity for the generativity, creativity, and empowerment that we spoke about before when we explored the nature of passion, provided only that you understand the importance of loving in real time, or in the moment.

This actually could also be true of ordinary relationships, in a slightly different way. Consider the roles you play in your other relationships. Because they are clear and easily identifiable, they can and do provide security, familiarity, and stability. But they can also allow a kind of freedom of creativity, albeit within certain specified boundaries. If you are not aware of the freedom you have, you can allow yourself to sink into a role; this can be a deadly trap for your creative self if you are not careful. You can sink into the very stagnation and inertia we spoke about in connection with passivity. How many times have you heard people speak about being "in a rut"? They may be speaking about their roles at work, their relationship roles, or the personality role they created for themselves. In all these cases, being in a rut is confining and imprisoning and indicates that they somehow forgot or are avoiding freedom and creativity.

Negative Stereotypes

In your love affair, you need to be especially careful not to let yourself "get into a rut" in your relationship role as the lover of a married person. This is because even though there are no particularly pleasant names for the role you occupy, your peers will try to make sure that you fully inhabit the unpleasant ones. This is because society is threatened by the freedom of choice you demonstrate in breaking away from its expectations and is eager to create a role that it can safely fit you into. This role is typically characterized by the negative stereotypes we discussed, so that you will not ever misunderstand your "outsider" position in relation to your peers, who are "living a normal life and doing things right." It is vitally important that you not take this personally, that you do not imagine that you really have done something to deserve the unpleasant characterizations that you may hear or sense in reference to you. You are living an unusual life and experiencing an uncommon love; it is natural for those who fear or do not understand your situation to try to make sense of it for themselves in whatever way they can. Unfortunately, it feels deeply unpleasant to be on the receiving end of such efforts.

Romantic Stereotypes

Further, negative stereotypes aren't the only ones you have to deal with. Another more subtle way society can keep you aware of your so-called illegitimacy is to create a romantic stereotype about the exciting and passionate life you are leading in contrast to everyone else's humdrum existence. While your love affair may indeed be deeply romantic, in this case "romantic" may be just their code word for "unrealistic" – your peers may wish you to understand that you are living a fantasy life that has nothing to do with their reality. This is another way that society protects itself against you –by making you and everyone else believe you are living a childlike dream, and that you are, by extension, a child and not a grown-up. Again, remember that your love affair often makes other people deeply uneasy as they struggle to create an explanatory framework for it. The characterization of you as a child, or of your love affair as "romantic" in the sense of "unrealistic," is another way that these mysterious elements can be safely incorporated into understanding.

Your Lover's Interest

Your married lover also may have an interest in seeing you safely established in a role of society's creation – the predator, mistress, homewrecker, dependent, needy, or pathological person who can't sustain a normal love relationship. If you come to believe any of these characterizations about yourself, perhaps you won't be so quick to give up the half a loaf he or she is offering you, which is understood to be better than none.

One may ask how this is different from the interest any one of us has in imprisoning our loved ones in roles that bind them to us. Perhaps it is not so different; however, the context of love affairs is so vastly different from the contexts of almost all other relationships that this commonplace practice assumes more significant and even sinister overtones in this case. Remember the most important differences between love affairs and other relationships; love affairs are typically secret, while other relationships are open and public, and love affairs also have deep structural imbalances built in which foster personal fragmentation and powerlessness. In addition, the particular role-prisons we are speaking about in love affairs are almost always negative for the single partner, making them extremely dangerous to the self-respect of an already fragile individual.

Why does your lover wish to see you safely established in one of these negative roles? Perhaps it is because you are both exchanging subliminal messages. Recall your lover's: "I may be as capable of betraying you as I have my spouse." In return, the message you are sending may be: "I am free enough from social constraints to risk the severe displeasure of family, friends, and community to engage in a love relationship that none of them approves of." The implication of your message is that you might also be free enough not to want to remain with your lover in an unbalanced and unfair relationship, once you see it for what it actually is. Therefore, it is in your lover's interest to keep you off-balance and subservient to what seems to be a necessary unfairness. Encouraging you to inhabit, to believe in, the various stereotypes of your ambiguous role is an effective way of doing this.

If this doesn't work, or if your lover is sensitive and kind-hearted and rejects these stereotypes on your behalf, another common way of keeping you in the affair is to suggest that you will not get this sort of deep, passionate love from anyone else – a manipulation that is extremely effective because, as we saw earlier, it may very well be true.

Again, note that none of these motivations is conscious, either from your community or from your lover. People usually sincerely believe they are acting in good faith toward you and have your best interests at heart. Their maneuverings are typically deeply unconscious — fully natural and understandable responses to those who are out of the ordinary and who color, so to speak, outside the lines. The impulse from *society* is to get you back into the fold, to live the same "normal" life that everyone else is living, so that no one else gets the same ideas as you. It is a deep and powerful civic or social impulse toward stability and security. However, the impulse from your *lover* opposes society's drive to return you to the fold; your lover's interest is to keep you in the affair, obedient to apparently necessary restraints and restrictions, so that you remain habituated to passivity and don't get any ideas of rebellion or freedom. It is a deep and powerful human impulse toward possession without responsibility.

What you need to do for yourself is to recognize both the inside and outside forces that are working against your being comfortable, whole, and happy in your affair. This is why we emphasized the role of the Observer — it is your Observing Self who can recognize these forces for what they are, and neither repress them from consciousness nor buy into them unreflectively.

Boundaries

We've spent some time considering the fragmentation of personhood that may come about very naturally in a love relationship such as this. We have also considered the issue of the passivity that can easily follow, and just now we looked at the issue of time and of living in the here and now.

How to put all these factors together to become a more healthy and generative being? Let's begin by looking at boundaries. We saw that one of the causes of fragmentation is the fact that the partners' respective personal boundaries are also deeply unbalanced in love affairs. We mentioned some of the ways this manifests itself – for example, your lover can call you, but you can't call back; your lover can come to your place but you can't go to his or her house, and so on. It appeared at first glance that this sort of thing was necessary just by the very nature of the practical logistics of the relationship.

Notice that what this actually means for our purposes is that your boundaries are expected to be open, flexible, and permeable but that your lover's boundaries are expected and permitted to be rigidly controlled and in fact to a certain extent tightly closed. Can this imbalance be changed?

In addition, your fragmentation is very literally a division of your usually integrated self into several pieces. In this case, instead of having one boundary, you potentially have several. It is hard enough to maintain clarity about your boundaries when you are whole and integrated; it is even more difficult to do so when you are in pieces. For example, how can you realistically expect to maintain a boundary between your mind and your heart? Yet it seems that you have to do so in order to maintain your participation in your affair. Therefore, it becomes very easy to abandon the thought of boundaries altogether. However, living and loving in real time means, above all, that you *must* understand yourself as having realistic and healthy boundaries. As far as time is concerned, we saw that this means a boundary between the present moment and both the past and the future – this gives you a freshness of experience in the moment that is of great value in focusing your attention and seeing yourself as integrated and whole. As far as your personhood is concerned, it means that you must begin to regard yourself as integrated and whole, and not scattered into pieces that have no definable shape.

How can this be accomplished? First of all, try asking yourself, in the moment, what it is that you actually want from this relationship. Notice I don't say "What do you wish for?" – obviously, what you wish for is for everything suddenly and magically to work out to normalize the relationship; you and your lover go off into the sunset and live happily ever after and you don't have to worry about any of this any more. This is wishful thinking and probably is not going to happen. The more difficult question is, given the situation *as it is*, what is it that you actually want?

All the exercises you have done so far in this and the other two sections have had as one of their primary goals the re-establishment of your freedom – freedom from obsessive thinking, freedom from the emotional roller coaster, freedom from the tyranny of expectations, fears, and stereotypes, freedom from illusion. Here is another exercise, one that will focus your attention even more on the whole, integrated person who is you. You may find this one extremely difficult to do.

Exercise 9

Knowing What You Actually Want

Return to your notebook to do this very simple written exercise. I say this is a simple exercise, and it is, but it is very definitely not an easy one. In this exercise, you will learn to separate what you realistically want, now, from what you unrealistically wish for, in the future-based-on-your-expectations-based-on-your-memories.

• Write down, in simple, short sentences exactly what it is that you want. This must be something possible and pertaining to you alone (we all "want" to win the lottery). Remember that the only thing that you are sure is possible for you is what will come from within you – you have very little, if any, control over what comes to you from outside. But you **can** control and direct what comes to you from inside yourself.

• Once again, there will be a strong temptation to edit, only this time you will be tempted to shape what you want to what you think you can get. Do not allow yourself to do this. This is not about what you think you can get; it is not about your circumstances (your love affair and its social and emotional difficulties) nor about anyone else who is part of those circumstances (your lover and his or her apparently fixed needs, your community of friends and relatives). This is about you and only you – what do you really want?

Comments:

In order to focus this exercise for you a little more precisely, I will tell you about a former psychotherapy client of mine from years ago. Lost and trapped in an unhappy and stagnant marriage, overweight from years of eating for comfort, depressed, apathetic and passive from too many disappointments, she had come to see me for "help." Eventually, after several weeks of fruitless meandering, where neither she nor I seemed to be getting any clarity on her situation, I asked her this question: "Well, what do you want?"

This simple question galvanized the psychotherapy and became a theme for many weeks to come, because she could not answer me. She did not even understand the question! She was so accustomed to not ever being able to get anything she wanted, she had literally *stopped wanting*, for years, and even had forgotten what it felt like to want anything at all. (Recall the previous discussion of outsmarting deprivation by learning to want less. Recall also Epictetus admonishing us to "want events to happen as they do happen"; this woman's situation is a possible outcome of such learning not to want.) This became the focus of our work for the next several weeks – re-learning what it felt like to be a person who wanted things and re-learning what those things were.

Is this you? Can you state clearly what you want? The truth is that many of us may have trouble answering this powerful question truthfully, completely, or adequately. For persons who are involved in love affairs, however, it is often an even more excruciatingly difficult task. If you are having difficulty identifying what you want, this is probably a boundary problem. It means that it is likely that there are so many pieces of you scattered around, the boundaries of those pieces are so loose and porous, and passivity has for so long been the hallmark of your being, that there may not even be much of a *you* at this point to want anything at all. Rather than regarding all this attention to yourself as somehow too selfish or self-centered, consider the opposite situation – that "you" may hardly be there at all.

A third exercise will make the problem somewhat clearer.

Exercise 10

Re-creating Your Self

We spoke about creating your Self when we were looking at the dangers of getting "into a rut" in relationships, and we noted that you were in a circumstance where you were in fact free to do just that – the other side of the coin of not having socially approved roles to inhabit. Now this exercise asks you to do so – to create your Self. Go back to your notebook and answer the following questions:

- How can I become whole, integrated, free of stereotypes and unrealistic expectations, living in the moment, experiencing emotion authentically, and able to know what I want? What kind of person do I need to be? What do I need to change about myself?

Do I need to change my pre-conceived ideas, my reflexive feelings, my narrow vision?

- What new personality structures would I have to create for myself? Do I need to be more (less) sensitive, more (less) analytic? Should I be more assertive, less aggressive?

- What **old** personality habits would I have to shed? Should I be less obedient, less passive and unreflective? Should I be **more** accommodating, more charitable, more tolerant?

- What is my true self after all? Who am I really? Who do I want to be?

Comments:

Here, you will be literally creating your Self. You, not society or your lover, will be the judge and the guide of who your Self really is; your Observing Self and your experiencing self can finally come together to create the loving, generative, wise, and exciting person who is the true you. And furthermore, this person – you – will have firm and clear boundaries; will be free of "baggage"; will be out of reach of both society's and your lover's manipulations; and will be in the present moment and living it fully, on your own terms and responsive to your own needs.

Recall that in Exercise 8 you were asked to focus on an imaginary or remembered lovemaking experience. The chances are that passionate love is or has been a key element in your affair, something that may have gotten you into it in the first place and, among other things, kept you in it, perhaps for years. It is useful, then, to continue to focus on the attention to the moment that you experience in lovemaking as an example of the kind of attention that you want to achieve for yourself in your relationship as a whole and for most of the rest of your life as well. You can regard this, in a sense, as "making love" with the rest of your life. For right now, attend to the moment that is being asked of you: with full attention, create or re-create your true Self.

Notice also that as you learn your Self and your true boundaries, another effect of this is to make you more active and less passive. Suddenly you know some of what you want, and you feel yourself entitled to want it; this can significantly change the active-passive dynamic in your relationship. And notice your feeling of empowerment. Your creation of your own self has made you more powerful to make changes in the structure of your relationship – you do not always need to be on the downside of its structural imbalances.

Can you also "eat your cake and have it too"? In other words, can you have passionate love in the context of a very difficult and illicit relationship and still be free to act, to decide, to choose, to design your own life? Remember that this is part of what it means to be able to perform "effective action." Do you have what it takes to navigate all the dangers and pitfalls of a love affair without fragmenting yourself and losing your boundaries? At this point, you should be able to imagine eventually answering "yes" to that question.

Realistically, it should also be noted that these exercises may have awakened you to a realization that you do *not* actually want to be in such a relationship after all, and they may have given you the freedom and strength to withdraw from it, if that is what you wish. The difference between leaving the affair now, rather than earlier, is that now you are not running away in fear, bitterness, or depression; you are not escaping from anything. Now you are making a conscious, rational decision based on what you have learned about yourself and about who you are, and you are leaving without blame, fingerpointing, or resentment. You are able to respect your partner and honor the deeply important experience you have both been through while choosing to live a life free of its particular stresses on your mind and heart.

Here is a final exercise that you can do with your partner, one that may give you a fresh perspective on your love affair and will let you know something of how your lover perceives the issue of boundaries.

Exercise 11

Double Exposure

On the surface, this is another playful sex exercise, a written one this time, but it is geared to have each of you learn something very useful about your relationship and how each of you sees it and yourselves.

- After you have had a particularly intense and rewarding sexual experience together, each of you might take some time during the week that follows to write about it.

- Describe what happened in detail – where you were; who did what to whom, what it felt like; what you saw, heard, felt, experienced; what you thought about; what the quality of the air and light were; whether the atmosphere changed; and so on.

- Be extremely explicit and graphic. Describe it as if you

had to make someone else "see" exactly what happened, so that someone else could have a vicarious experience similar to yours while reading it. Do not hold back your descriptions of the experience on the grounds of shyness or modesty.

▪ When each of you has done this, read each other's work. You will find this very enjoyable and maybe even exciting, but you may also be very surprised at what you learn about yourselves and each other.

Comments:

Here is an example of a surprise that one couple received when they did this exercise. It turns out that the unattached partner wrote it in the second person – in other words, it was written almost as a letter to the other partner, using "you" and "I" as the main pronouns. The married partner wrote it entirely in the third person – in other words, as if the description were about two other people, using "he," "she," and "they" as the main pronouns. Does this suggest anything to you about the respective ways in which they viewed their relationship? It certainly gave them tremendous food for thought. A very informative way to use this exercise is to do it twice, once before you implement some of the suggestions in these pages and once after. You might see some deep and definite changes in yourself and in your attitudes toward your uncommon love relationship.

The Next Step

Now that you are beginning to have your proper boundaries in place and know something of how your lover regards the boundary issue in your relationship, how does this affect your actual participation in your affair? The first thing to recognize is that you have assumed a more equal status in your relationship; you can now take on more of a guiding role. We will speak more about how actually to do this later on. The second thing, interestingly enough, is that you now have certain clear *obligations* to your partner and to your affair, obligations which flow from that new status of equality.

Etiquette and Protocol

It is extremely important to recognize that equality works both ways; your partner must also be recognized as having boundaries that are legitimate under the circumstances and which should not be breached by you. However, the reason for your respect for his or her boundaries is now different from the reasons that were in place before. Earlier, you were in a position of feeling that you were in some sense trapped by the demands of your lover's life style, and there was a sense that there was nothing you could do about it – you had to "take it or leave it," as it were. This trapped feeling was part of what led to fragmentation and emotional conflict. Now, with your recognition of both of you as persons in your own right, you are no longer trapped, but this recognition now requires you to make some adjustments in how you deal with the boundaries your lover has brought into the relationship.

It means a recognition that he or she has rights, just as you do. Specifically, your lover has a right to construct his or her life exactly as he or she pleases – this means that if your lover wants to live a life that includes both a marriage and a love affair, your lover has every right to do so.

You, in turn, have every right either to agree to this situation or to walk away. This is what that original agreement between you and your partner actually means – not just a passive acquiescence to an unfortunate set of circumstances that your partner wishes to characterize as unavoidable, but an active recognition of the freedom and integrity of *both* parties to the agreement, which by definition includes an active recognition of *each* person's rights.

You have a right to require that you be treated with the dignity and respect that is due you as a free person who has chosen his or her own life path. What you do *not* have a right to do is to demand explanations of your lover, harass or persuade your married partner into leaving his or her marriage, call your lover at home, make your relationship known to your lover's spouse, bluff your partner, or anything else of that sort. This means recognizing your lover's rights, as painful and difficult as that recognition may be. Let's take these issues one by one.

Demanding Explanations

Your lover does not owe you any explanations of why he or she made the choice to continue a marriage while pursuing an affair with you. Here is why this sounds counter-intuitive.

Recall that in this and earlier sections, we had discussed the division and conflict between your mind and your heart – your heart "knows" that love has its own imperatives, and that it is in some sense a violation of love to allow this kind of situation to exist. It seems intuitively clear that if you love someone, you make any sacrifices necessary to honor that love, even if it means giving up the security of a long-established marriage, with all the comforts and privileges that go along with it. This is what your heart "knows," and the fact is, your heart is right. That *is* what love means – usually.

In your particular case, your mind tried to put the brakes on your heart by reminding it that you have no ultimate choices in this matter, that you have to take or leave the situation as it is, and that the situation itself is not ever going to change. But your heart responded with its usual pattern of hope and wishful thinking, and you were immediately at war with yourself.

However, now that you understand the importance of your own boundaries, your mind and heart can be reconciled; your decision to respect your lover's boundaries is an active, conscious choice, based on your clarity and sense of self. It is literally none of your business why your lover chooses to live such a lifestyle, and furthermore it is no longer your problem. Your lover's correct answer to the question "Why?" is "Because that's what I want to do." There is nothing further to be said. It has always been up to you to decide whether such a relationship is acceptable to you – if not, it is then up to you to withdraw.

All this may seem shocking, counterintuitive, and lacking in compassion. We have looked deeply and in detail at a love relationship that is or has become structured explicitly to satisfy the needs of only one of its partners, and we have seen with perhaps chilling clarity how that structure can damage and injure the other partner. In fact, this entire book is built around trying to alleviate and heal some of this damage. Why, then, would I seem to be discouraging you from looking at the morality of what your partner is doing and asking for an explanation? If a common-sense understanding of immorality includes "the deliberate injury of another in order solely to satisfy one's own self-interest," does it not seem self-evident that your married lover is behaving immorally? And should this not be acknowledged, at least in passing? The assumptions I made in the beginning of this book may now seem too simplistic; isn't the effort at non-judgementalism immoral in its own right? Perhaps you have the right to a more satisfying answer to the question "Why?", an answer that requires your partner to account for himself or herself morally, rather than merely taking refuge behind boundaries of privacy.

Clearly it is true that moral issues play a deep role in love affairs, as will be seen from a slightly different angle in the final section of this book, and I have no wish to discourage evaluations that are bound to arise as you contemplate the various moral and ethical elements of your affair. However, the orientation of this particular exploration of affairs is to provide means for the clarity and understanding that must *precede* moral evaluation, part of which requires seeing your affair "as is." Early in an affair it becomes brutally clear that only one of its partners has the power to change its essential nature, and thereby its name, its structure, and the expectations and obligations of the partners. This, as we saw, is unlikely to happen; meanwhile, the structure of the love affair is what it is from the very beginning. Whatever immorality may be contained and expressed in love affairs, it has its focus and origin right at the beginning, from which it informs and suffuses other events and experiences in the relationship.

Therefore, if you determine that your lover is living an immoral life, and if your decisions about remaining in your love affair are structured around morality, then you need to recognize that you are probably dealing with an all-or-nothing situation. If you stay in, you are in effect accepting and in fact participating in whatever immorality you believe your lover is expressing; on the other hand, if you reject his or her immorality and wish to behave morally yourself, then it seems you are obliged to withdraw from the relationship altogether, or never even enter into it in the first place. It stands to reason that a decision based on moral evaluation happens quite early in a love affair, or even precedes it. Having agreed to participate on an ongoing basis, the issue of who is or is not behaving immorally in this fundamental sense is irrelevant – the love affair simply is what it is. The problem now becomes how to live with your initial decision or on what grounds now to decide otherwise, rather than how to judge the situation, your lover, and yourself morally.

Harassing or Persuading Your Lover to Leave His or Her Marriage

For similar reasons of privacy and respect for your lover's autonomy, it is illegitimate for you to imagine that you know what is best for your lover, namely to leave the marriage and begin a new life with you. It has occasionally happened that a married person will leave the marriage and begin a life with his or her lover, but this is a rare act of courage, clarity, and integrity and not normally to be expected. (This is particularly true if your love affair did not come about accidentally, if your married lover is a person who actively seeks out extramarital relationships as a chosen life style.) If such a choice is made, it must be your lover's autonomous and free choice.*

Besides the fact that it is disrespectful of your lover for you to harass or persuade him or her, it is not a good idea in general. You might be able to coerce your partner into such a course of action, using either persuasive logic or emotional blackmail based on guilt, but because it was not your partner's free choice, it will backfire sooner or later. Your lover will grow to resent you and eventually even to hate you, as he or she realizes what has been given up in order to appease you. Again, the important recognition here is that, just as you are free to choose things for your life, your lover is free also, and this freedom must be respected. It is what a person's autonomy actually amounts to – the right to make choices for his or her life.

This is actually not specific just to love affairs – people very often think that they know what is best for those they love and will do everything in their power to make these "best" things happen. A particularly commonplace example is parents who decide what their children ought to do with their lives – what their major in college should be, for instance – then implement their wishes by threatening to withhold funds for tuition if the child should decide differently. Such actions usually have destructive effects.

---

* At this point, one may wonder at the contrast between a lover who has the "courage, clarity, and integrity" to honor fully the love he or she feels, at whatever cost, and the implied lack of these qualities in a lover who does not choose to take this action. What, one might ask, am I doing loving a person who is seemingly without these qualities? The reasons for loving someone are varied and mysterious, and usually cannot be understood analytically. The French philosopher Montaigne recognized this and offers, helpfully, "...because it was he, because it was I." ("Of Friendship", in Pakaluk, *Other Selves*.)

Calling Your Lover at Home

Again, this is part and parcel of respecting your lover as a person, which means respecting his or her privacy and freedom to make life choices. By invading the marital home, you are implying that your lover does not have the right to privacy and that *you* will determine whether his or her boundaries ought to be respected. And again, for the same reasons as above, this is likely to backfire, only more quickly.

Making Your Affair Known to the Spouse

For all the reasons mentioned above, taking matters into your own hands in this way shows a disrespect for your lover's autonomy and right to decide his or her own life, as well as a discourtesy that betrays your lack of sensitivity to these issues. In addition, it shows a shabby "get even" mentality that should not be part of your own free personhood. A free person in a love affair does not imagine that he or she has anything to get even for. Your lover has not wronged you, and moreover, your lover's spouse has not done anything to you to warrant this sort of harmful intervention in both their lives. If there are young children involved, you could be ruining several lives in addition to your lover's and his or her spouse's.

Bluffing

This is a very immature and also dangerous undertaking. A typical bluff is to set an ultimatum – "If you haven't done this thing I ask by March 31, I'm walking out." There is an assumption, usually erroneous, that this will be enough to get the action that you want.

Here it is important to recognize the difference between a genuine deadline and an ultimatum. If you, as a free person, have decided for yourself that you honestly cannot pursue this relationship in its present form beyond a certain time limit, that is one thing. That is an authentic effort to make your needs known to your partner and to inform him or her that you are prepared to take action to preserve yourself. Your partner is entitled to know how you feel and what the consequences of how you feel might be. An ultimatum, on the other hand, is a threatening and coercive manipulation, especially if you do not really mean it. It says to your partner that you feel entitled to force him or her to do something he or she does not really want to do – a blatant disrespect of your partner as a person.

Moreover, it implies that you assume your own status in your partner's life to be more important than everything your lover will have to sacrifice in order to be with you – this simply may not be true. Breaking up an established family, especially if there are children involved, is a hard thing to ask of anyone; moreover, the allures of property, established domestic rhythms, familiarity, and emotional security should not be underestimated. Next to those powerful incentives to maintain the status quo, a love affair simply pales in luster and importance when it is time actually to choose.

Last, if it is a bluff and if you simply assume that you *are* important in this way, and your lover does not come through, you have been taught a painful lesson; you now have clear proof that you are *not* important enough to warrant such sacrifice. In addition, you now have to put up or shut up – either follow through on your threat, or back down. Because it was a bluff, and your partner called your bluff, this translates into either "cutting off your nose to spite your face," or losing both power and credibility in your relationship. At that point, if you decide to stay, it will be more difficult to have your partner respect your free personhood – you have shown unmistakably that you are not free, that you feel childish games are the proper adult way to get what you want.

Freedom and Responsibility

As you see, freedom brings the responsibility to recognize the Other also as a free person who has rights. Moreover, by respecting yourself as a free person who has the right to make choices and the right to make your legitimate needs known to your partner, you see that you are not thereby automatically given license to do or get anything you want. This is a subtle and important point. Making your needs known does not automatically require your partner to fulfill those needs; at some point, what is needed is serious and respectful negotiation between the two of you. If you feel that some of your needs are non-negotiable, *you* must decide either to remain in a relationship which does not satisfy you or to leave. It is not a decision for you to force your *lover* to make.

As we saw in the discussion of loving here and now, a love affair is not structured around the usual imperatives of love in the way an ordinary love relationship might be and usually is, with love and its consequences carrying over into the rest of your life. This is an incorrect perspective that generates unrealistic expectations. Therefore, if a love relationship cannot be structured around the imperatives of love, it has to be structured around something else, and that something must be the imperatives of equality, of your equality with your lover as a person. And, as we see, such equality generates not only power for you but also responsibility.

This is the only way a love affair can be conducted with reasonable expectations and with respect for each other. Any effort to change forcibly the built-in structural imbalances of the relationship by any of the above inauthentic and dishonest means is eventually going to destroy the relationship altogether. The structural imbalances remain until and unless your lover decides to change them on his or her own, or until the two of you re-negotiate them to provide a more equitable proportion – they are characteristic of love affairs. The dynamic of power can be shifted as well, once you collect your fragmented pieces into a whole and begin to assert yourself as a person who is entitled to want, to need, and to make those wants and needs known, to yourself as well as to your partner.

In the fourth and final section, we will look at some of the actual events and issues that occur in love affairs, and we will try to get a sense of how your newly integrated, whole, and free self can make rational and ethical decisions about these issues, decisions that respect both your partner and yourself. Love affairs do share some common characteristics with other kinds of relationships. After all, there are two unique people involved, each of whom has his or her own needs, tastes, and personality characteristics. There is bound to be friction in the negotiation of ordinary issues – for example, how to spend the limited amount of time that you have together. There are also larger and more serious issues that pertain to love affairs in particular – for example, how to understand concepts like fidelity or loyalty in such a context. Are you, the unattached partner, free to have another love interest in your life at the same time as you are conducting your love affair? We will look at these and other issues in detail.

2701 Santa Rosa Ave.

Altadena. CA 91101

11:48 ~ 1:00

3 mi. 1st slight

3 ~ 20 sec.

21 ~ 42

43 - 60 | 30

IV
Changing Your Life

I n previous sections, we have looked at a broad range
of issues relating to having a love affair with a married
person. We saw how such a relationship tends to frag-
ment the Self or personhood of the unattached partner,
what personhood actually is and why it is important both
in love relationships and in the rest of life, and how you
can begin to re-acquaint yourself with who you actually
are through the written exercises that were provided.
The exercises in the first section focused on defining and
recognizing your Self and on strengthening your powers
of detached observation of your life and its issues.

Later, we saw how the built-in imbalances and unfair-
nesses in the structure and dynamics of a love affair work
to encourage the unattached partner into both fragmentation and passivity. We examined issues of powerlessness, justice, "citizenship," and integrity, and saw how

love affairs, by their very nature, can operate to the unattached partner's disadvantage in all these areas. The exercises in Part II used the tool of the Observing Self to focus on separating truth from illusion in your relationship with your lover.

In the third section, we took a closer look at passivity and then dealt with issues of time, boundaries, and perspective. In those exercises, you began the process of regrouping into a whole person who can be active rather than passive, focused rather than diffused, and clear rather than confused. The exercises here used the knowledge you gained in the first two sections to begin to re-integrate the various parts of your Self into a whole person, and, through the use of sexual fantasy, to begin to recognize your partner as an equal in this affair as well.

Now, we are going to confront the issue of actually changing your life. In this section, we will look at three authentic choices that are now possible for you in your relationship: how to leave with dignity, how to stay with integrity, and a third option – "The Pretzel."

It is likely that by now you have some intuitive sense of whether you want to stay or to go. This intuition may be very vague, but you might be experiencing it as a definite "pull" in one direction or another, perhaps combined with some feelings of fear and anxiety as you contemplate the unknown. Here are some considerations to sharpen decision-making and, for all these options, to lay out some of your possible fears for closer examination.

How To Leave With Dignity

Assessment

The first thing to do, armed with the knowledge and tools you have acquired from the discussions and exercises of the first three sections, is to make an honest, objective assessment of your situation. You will need to re-examine your relationship and confront all its advantages and disadvantages head-on: its love and passion, its unfairness and injustice, its intensity. You will also have to re-examine your emotional state: the "roller coaster," the contradictions of love and hate, whether your emotions are authentic or inauthentic, the glory and excitement of your life. Further, you will have to consider your mental state: the confusions, the contradictions of beliefs and values, the obsessive nature of your thinking.

In short, you will have to review all the self-evaluation you have been doing in the exercises in the previous sections. If this sounds suspiciously like a cost/benefit analysis, that is because it is exactly that. If you are already leaning in the direction of ending your affair, but find yourself hesitating, a cost/benefit analysis may be precisely what is needed to help organize the benefits and disadvantages of your choice more clearly.

Deciding to Leave

If you decide that you really do not wish to be involved in your love affair any longer, there are consequences that you are going to want to be prepared for. (Note: I am assuming that love is still present. If you have actually stopped loving your partner, it will not be as difficult for you to make this choice and your adjustment period will be milder and less painful. But please understand that leaving any familiar situation, no matter how uncomfortable, typically requires some adjustment.)

Love and passion are what we live for, but as we have seen, in the context of a love affair they can be dangerous. However, while leaving them behind can indeed be safer, it can also be very cold and very lonely without them. Here are some things you can expect to experience.

• On The One Hand . . .
You will feel like you lost an arm or a leg. Your familiar emotional and mental world will collapse overnight. All the things you are accustomed to have in your mind and in your heart will no longer have any place there, but you will continue to feel them anyway for some time to come – a little like the reputed "phantom pain" that remains when one actually does lose a limb.

You will have the taste of ashes in your heart. You will confront the prospect of what you imagine to be the barrenness of your life from that moment forward; your imagination will become your worst enemy as you take a long and chilling look into future loneliness and darkness. And do not think I am exaggerating for literary effect – these are precisely the kinds of dramatic feelings you are likely to have and that many people do report having.

It is important not to avoid this painful time, but to be prepared to experience it and to confront it directly. Otherwise, if you are not prepared, you may find yourself running back into the affair simply to escape the pain. As we saw before, decisions made simply to escape from something are not as effective as decisions made consciously and carefully from the perspective of a free person. Also, if you try to avoid it or distract yourself from the pain, it will only be there waiting for you some other time anyway, but then it will sneak up on you and take you by surprise. Better to meet it with full consciousness in the first place.

You can expect a long re-adjustment period characterized by these feelings and thoughts, depending on the length of the relationship and on the depth of emotion and passion you have experienced within it.

• On The Other Hand . . .

As time goes by – and it will, I promise you – you will begin to experience a gradually increasing sense of calmness and self-mastery. Your strength will begin to re-assert itself, very slowly, and as it does, you will begin to experience greater peace of mind and quietness of heart.

You will have an increasing clarity of thought and things will arrange themselves gradually into their proper perspective. Your emotional intensity will be gradually leveled out. You will be off the "roller coaster" and out of the depths of raging sorrow that you were in immediately after leaving your affair. You will also find your emotions and your thoughts assuming their authentic quality: for example, depression will be gradually replaced by genuine sorrow; obsession will give way to clear-eyed contemplation.

You may not experience all of these things or even any of them. These are the most common experiences that people report having, and it is wise to look at them carefully and be prepared for the likelihood that you may experience some of them too.

If You Change Your Mind

It often happens in love affairs that the unattached partner will end the relationship, only to have second thoughts and cold feet when it is actually time to live in a newly independent life. Returning to the affair could work out perfectly well, and it has for some. On the other hand, it may not, and there are common experiences that you should be prepared to face.

Things may not be the same after you re-establish your love affair. There may be either reduced or increased passion and emotional intensity; mutual fears and desires may consciously or unconsciously work to change the dynamics of the relationship; each of you may become more manipulative because of your respective fears and desires; your lover may be cautious and withdrawn, perhaps not too giving because he or she is afraid to be hurt again.

There may be a significant shift in the balance of power in the relationship. Either of you might experience a reduction or an increase in your power as your perceptions of each other change; as, for example, one or both of you see the other as "in the wrong."

You may find it either easier or harder to get out the next time. It may be "easier" because you have already done it once, and yet the relationship survived; therefore, the stakes are lowered and you might feel more ready to do it once more, thinking you can come back again if it doesn't work out. On the other hand, it might be "harder" because you have experienced the cold and lonely world outside of your lover's arms, and might not be in a hurry to experience that again, no matter how painful the relationship becomes.

Finally, there is the issue of fairness to your lover. After all, your lover also had to get used to life without you and this may have been difficult. Now your lover has to get used to having you back. If you leave and come back too often, the uncertainty may eventually inspire your *partner* to end the relationship – the decision may be taken out of your hands.

How To Leave

• Keeping Your Partner Informed

As we saw in the last section, once you regain your wholeness and integrity – your personhood – it is important to recognize your partner as a whole person too. We saw that this recognition of your own freedom brings with it recognition of your responsibilities and obligations to your lover as well.

A primary obligation in this case is to keep your partner informed of your fears, desires, thoughts, and intentions. This is a very delicate undertaking. The temptation to use these things against your lover in a manipulative or punishing way is very great, especially if you have not mastered your anger. What is needed is to recognize the line between information that is manipulative – making your partner react in some pre-planned way to satisfy your own needs – and information that you owe to your partner as your friend and lover, so you do not take him or her completely by surprise when you leave the relationship. Your partner has a right to have advance notice that you are not happy and that you are considering leaving the relationship. In this way, he or she can prepare and plan for a future without you, in case you do follow through with your intentions.

Again, it is vital not to use these expressions of your intentions as a threat or a bluff. As we saw, doing so diminishes your own personhood and causes your partner to lose respect for you when these manipulations become obvious.

- **Asking for Help from Your Partner**
Your lover has the same right to try to make things right in your affair as he or she would have in an ordinary love relationship or a friendship or a marriage. It is possible that your partner may come up with changes or new ideas that would be acceptable to you; you have an obligation to let him or her try.

Moreover, this may be the first time that your partner has ever really stopped to think about the kind of difficulties that such a relationship imposes on the unattached partner. Insight is valuable; asking for help gives your partner the opportunity for such insight and is worthwhile for its own sake, even if it doesn't save the affair.

- **Walking Away Gracefully**
When all else fails and your honest assessment of the situation so indicates, walk away gracefully and with full sensitivity to both your partner's grief and your own.

Have the courage to do so in person, not by letter or by leaving a telephone message on the answering machine. You will of course be facing a painful and difficult time while your partner assimilates the devastating news. Have enough respect for your partner and for the love affair you shared to take your leave in person.

Allow your lover to be angry, hurt, or sorrowful, even if

you think he or she has no justification or warrant for these feelings. Deal authentically with your lover's bereavement – because that is exactly what it is – and be honest enough to acknowledge your own. This is not the time for "getting even" or "now you know how it feels" or whatever other ideas may come from any part of you that is still angry. It is a time for honoring the important, vital, and beautiful experience you have both been through, and a time for healing and tenderness as you say goodbye.

How To Stay With Integrity

Assessment

If you are leaning in the direction of trying to continue your affair, to stay in, you are again going to need the same kind of cost/benefit assessment of your situation as before. Here, however, because your intuitions are telling you to try to stay, you need to look not only at the fears you might be experiencing, but also very closely at the nature of love. We will consider three different kinds of love, and you can ask yourself whether one or several of these apply to what you are feeling while you contemplate this decision.

Deciding to Stay

If you decide to stay, it might be a bit more difficult to find clarity. At this point in your decision-making process, there are two different ways that you can end up staying in your relationship.

• Deferring Your Decision

One way is by deferring any decision for now. This can mean one of two things. Either you are still working through your assessment process and have in fact made a genuine decision to "wait and see," or you are feeling paralyzed and unable actually and firmly to decide one way or another. In the second instance, you end up staying in somewhat by default.

If you are genuinely still working through your decision and need more time, this is a wise and cautious resistance to making an impulsive or reflexive choice. It is an extremely important decision, and you need to give yourself time to be as sure as possible that you are doing the right thing. Note that because you still love each other, it is unlikely that you will ever be *completely* sure that the decision you make now is the right one – you can only hope to be *mostly* sure.

On the other hand, if you are "defaulting" because you don't want to commit yourself to making a decision, this is an inauthentic response to having to make a decision that is important and perhaps even necessary for your well-being. If you are "stuck" between *yes* and *no*, and find yourself not really making a genuine effort to get unstuck, you are in danger of becoming passive again, of simply acquiescing to the status quo because it is too emotionally dangerous to make either choice.

This is a perfectly normal human reaction to being confronted with what looks like a "lose-lose" decision – just avoiding the whole thing as long as you can. However, if you allow it to go on too long, you risk gradually losing all the ground you have gained in becoming a whole, integrated person who acts freely and effectively in the world.

- **Actively Making the Decision to Stay**

Making an active decision to stay means that your commitment is deep enough and strong enough to meet the difficulties inherent in your relationship. The structure of it does not distract you, nor on the other hand is passionate love by itself enough to hold you. Your commitment is stronger than passion – you are committed to a *person*, and to a genuine friendship.

Eros, Filia, and Agape

The ancient Greeks customarily distinguished between three kinds of love.

Eros is the passionate love of desire, emotion, and sexuality. This probably has been the guiding dynamic of your love affair up until now. By itself, however, it typically does not provide a deep enough motivation to continue indefinitely a relationship that has so many disadvantages for one of its partners. Incidentally, it also docs not usually provide enough motivation to continue *any* relationship indefinitely – passion eventually dies if it feeds only on itself.

Filia is the deep, affectionate love of intimate friendship. This is the kind of love that can begin to transcend the great difficulties of a love affair. It is the love of the person for his or her own sake, and not just the essentially self-interested love of mere passion. It is the recognition of the partner as "another self"; it is the love that ultimately must underwrite passion, if passion is to survive and grow. It is the love that endures and that may, in fact, conquer all.

Agape is the third, and some say the highest, kind of love. It is traditionally understood as the universal love of God through your friend and through humankind in general. It is said also to work the other way around – to be the universal love of humankind and individual persons through your love of God. However, the presence of the God-principle need not prevent unbelievers from experiencing and understanding *agape*. In its pure form, it implies a wholeness and inclusiveness of love that embraces your particular friend as a special, exemplifying, and reflecting part of that wholeness, so that as you love your friend you are loving that which brought you together, however you might understand it. You can then also understand that the same force brought all of humankind to actuality, and your love becomes deeper and more meaningful on that level.

Your decision to remain in such a difficult relationship at this point must reflect the maturing of your mutual love beyond *eros* to include *filia,* and perhaps even *agape.* An important part of your assessment process must include your honest appraisal of whether both you and your partner have gone beyond *eros* in your love for one another. However, even if you decide that you have, your love affair does not then automatically become any easier to live with, so here are some suggestions and considerations to help smooth the way.

How to Stay

The primary requirement for you in continuing your love affair is absolute, clear-eyed honesty about all of its aspects. You will no longer have the luxury of story-telling, romanticizing, or obsessing about the kinds of issues we have been discussing. Only absolute clarity will help you maintain your bearings; none of the difficulties of your affair have disappeared or been lessened. What has changed is that you have grown in strength and knowledge.

• Accepting the Imbalances

First, it is clear that you must continue to accept many of the imbalances that are inherent in the structure of the relationship, but as you will see, it is possible to adjust some of them to reflect a more equal status with your lover. An extremely important point to bear in mind, however, not only for this relationship but for all others as well, is that you are *never* required to accept "dis-integrating" harm to yourself as a cost of either *eros*, *filia*, or *agape*.

It is true that many relationships are extremely painful for one reason or another – being the parent of a handi-capped child, being married to a mentally ill person, being the friend of an alcoholic or drug addict, and so on. But it is important to separate the unavoidable painful circumstances of a relationship from the unnecessary pain of personal fragmentation and damage to your Self; none of these painful relationships ought to require you to lose the boundaries of your personhood. If they do, this is due more to mistaken assumptions on the part of the participants in the relationship than to the painful circumstances themselves. Painful circumstances are less likely to cause you to lose your boundaries than are mis-taken assumptions about relationship roles. This applies especially to love affairs.

• Giving Your Lover What He or She Truly Wants

As humans, we share an amusing and ironic trait. While we live our lives in ways that indicate unmistakably the things we find truly important, we can simultaneously and with great sincerity and conviction pay lip service to other, conflicting priorities and ideals. Occasionally the world, taking us to be who our *actions* show us to be, gives us what it sees we truly want. And, ironically, we become confused and angry when this happens.

Your lover has constructed a life style that indicates his or her actual priorities very clearly, and you are not one of the highest. The priorities appear to be home, spouse, property, community, established comfortable rhythms of life, and so on, as discussed elsewhere. If you are going to be emotionally stable staying in your love affair, it is clear that you must reconcile yourself to this somewhat uncomfortable truth, but then you must turn around and reconstruct *your* priorities in the same way. You must make your lover as "secondary" in your priorities as you are in his or hers.

Note that I am not speaking of how you both feel about each other or how much time you spend thinking about each other; it is clear that if there is genuine love between you, that love permeates both of your hearts and minds at all times or at least most of the time. But this is different from what actually happens in your lives, as we saw earlier. Actual time devoted to or lived with each other is typically sparse and has the air of being "stolen" from other pursuits or persons.

To accomplish this reordering of your own priorities, you must perform the delicate balancing act of distancing yourself from your affair and your lover both mentally and emotionally in your life, without sacrificing genuineness and emotional immediacy when you *are* spending time with your lover.

In this way, you are quite literally and actually "listening" to your lover and giving your lover what he or she *actually wants* – a part-time, secondary, but deeply emotional and meaningful relationship. Your lover, of course, would not accept that characterization as what he or she really wants. In your lover's mind, what he or she "wants" is for you to consider yourself a full-time lover, a true soulmate who is necessarily bound by circumstances unfortunately beyond your lover's control, while he or she continues to live the full, dual life that in fact marginalizes you. Further, your lover wants you to believe that you are as important as or even more important than his or her actual spouse. But you cannot allow yourself to assent to any of this; such illusions and enchantments serve only to reinforce the imbalances and injustices we spoke about in earlier sections. This is why clarity of observation and thought is important here; passion, desire, and hope are always going to be alive in your heart as long as there is love. You need to protect yourself against these tendencies of your heart to take over your decision-making, which can get you into trouble.

• Accepting Aloneness

In order to separate yourself in this way, you need to accept the aloneness of your life, in the sense of not having a real mate, but without allowing yourself to slide into loneliness. You need to confront and to accept the reality that you are going to continue to live your life essentially alone or unattached. You are *not* part of a long-distance "couple," you are *not* "together," your lover is *not* your "mate." What you are is someone's beloved friend; what you do have is a well-loved friend of your own and an occasional charming companion whose company you enjoy and look forward to. Your lover needs to become no more important in your own life than any of your other dear friends or beloved family members. This requires you to maintain a delicate mental and emotional balance.

- **Taking Control of the "Schedule"**

To facilitate this, the frequency of your contacts, both in person and by telephone or letter, must not be dependent only on your lover's availability, although certainly that will continue to be a factor simply by the nature of things. You actively must adjust this frequency so that you can maintain your mental and emotional equilibrium while still continuing to have an important and meaningful love relationship under difficult circumstances. Too much frequency of contact may draw you once again into obsession and emotional chaos; too little contact does not honor the fullness of the love between you and may eventually lead to a fading-out of the relationship.

Note that if this fading-out is what you are actually hoping for so that you don't have to make a genuine decision and take responsibility for it, this may again be a passive-resistant and inauthentic response to having to choose, unless a gradual phase-out is something both you and your lover have openly agreed to.

- **Recognizing That Your Life Belongs to You**

You must begin to see your life as belonging to you and characterized primarily by things other than your affair: work, family, friends, culture, leisure, civic consciousness. Your love affair needs to become "normalized" in your everyday life as just another important element in that life, but not as the major element that drives it or as the only thing worth living for. This is a large part of the struggle to re-establish the balances of fairness and justice in your relationship.

• "Compartmentalizing" And Its Dangers

In this context, a word of caution is indicated. We spoke earlier about "living in the moment" and saw how important it is to avoid constantly bringing the past or the future into the present moment, at the expense of living that present moment to its fullest. We saw that a here-and-now orientation is important for genuineness and recognition of yourself and your partner as separate but whole persons.

But unless you are mindful, living in the moment in this way may easily allow the elements of your life to become *too* compartmentalized, sealed in airtight "compartments" in your consciousness, with rigid walls between them. While you need to be careful about allowing your emotions and thoughts about your affair to rule your life – to "carry over" too much – you need to be just as careful of this sort of locked-in rigidity. Rigid compartments are emphatically not the same sort of thing as clear personal boundaries.

You do not need to "compartmentalize" anything else in your life in this rigid sort of way. Your contacts with your family, friends, and colleagues are indeed separated in your mind and heart from one another, but only in a superficial and practical sort of way – for example, you would of course think and act somewhat differently with your 10-year-old child than with your boss at work.

In your other relationships, you naturally allow yourself to enjoy remembering an amusing moment or anticipating an interesting conversation, and your relationship with your lover should be no different – you can enjoy this sort of memory and anticipation in your affair, too. This is part of "normalizing" it in your life. The delicate task is to strike a balance between rigid compartmentalization and the complete diffusion of psychic boundaries characteristic of obsession, powerlessness, or total passivity.

These guidelines, while initially seeming to be very difficult to follow, will in fact allow you to begin to focus on *filia* in your affair as well as on *eros*. *Eros* does not by itself permit much distraction – remember our discussions of passionate love – but *filia*, the deep love characteristic of intimate friendship, is what will actually allow you to remain with an important relationship without losing your soul all over again.

If the relationship continues to deepen, then gradually *agape*, the love of the God-principle or a transcendent spiritual element through your partner, may become part of your passion and friendship as well, adding compassion, charity, and mercy to passionate and affectionate love and to the search for justice. This is the richest and most rewarding love; it is also permanent – a binding together of souls as well as bodies. In the context of a love affair, with all its internal and external problems, only exceptional mental and emotional strength and deep wisdom can carry this off. But it is possible, and also desirable. It is this depth of love and compassion that is characteristic of all abiding love between people, and it can be characteristic even of lovers in a love affair.

A Third Way, Affectionately Named "The Pretzel"

The above meditation on the dimensions of wisdom required to remain in an affair depends on one key element: complete acceptance of life lived alone, not "together" or as part of a "couple." As we said, exceptional mental and emotional strength is required to understand and to live this choice in this way, because the actual lived experience of being in love feels as though you *are* together, part of a couple. It takes constant mental discipline to maintain the correct Confucian understanding of the reality of this situation, but understanding that reality is the key to the depth of experience that can be achieved in your love affair.

But, let's face it – it is not easy to accept the requirement that in order to have *eros*, *filia*, or *agape* in 10% of your life, you must in effect sacrifice the other 90% by agreeing to live it alone. This returns us to the essential unfairness of a relationship such as this. It is likely that you also want a real mate – someone who is there for you and is prepared to fulfill the requirements of the citizenship of love and friendship; someone to spend your time with, to talk to, to go to the movies with, to entertain friends with, to take a walk with, to go on vacation with, to spend weekends with, to watch TV with, on a regular or even daily basis and not just once in a while.

You are entitled to want these things; being alone for a lifetime is not natural to humankind. Even if we are born alone and even if we do die alone, there does not seem to be any reason to believe that we are required to live alone.

There seems to be no reason why you need to accept such a demand on your life, particularly when your lover has made the choice to live a dual life and is not alone. He or she has both a lover and a mate, so there is no question of your lover living 90% of life alone. Why should you?

This is a vexed question, as you will see shortly. It requires careful consideration of the following important issues:

• **Sexual Aesthetics.** Some people can have ongoing sexual relationships with more than one person at a time; others cannot.

• **Ethics.** What are your obligations to your lover? Can you begin another relationship while still continuing your affair? What sort of obligations would you have to this other lover? Whom should you tell what to? Should you be secret about either or both of your relationships with the other partner, or should you be open? Are you prepared for the duplicity and lying that accompany secrecy?

• **Integrity and fragmentation.** Here you go again – mind against heart, mind against mind, only this time you are doing it to yourself.

• **The "State of the Union."** What will be the condition of your Self if you decide on this option? A life built on deception, no matter how justifiable, will have a tremendous impact on your personhood and its mental, emotional, and spiritual condition. Is it worth it?

And you *must choose.* If you stay in your love affair, you must choose between the obligation to yourself to live a full life, and the obligation to yourself and others to lead an ethical life. You cannot choose both because you cannot have both. Witness your lover's dual life; one cannot be both fulfilled *and* ethical in relationships built on lies and deceit. There may naturally be some hesitation here about the ethical nature of *your* participation in an extra-marital affair to begin with; after all, it might be argued that you are already behaving unethically, at least toward your lover's spouse, by participating in your lover's marital duplicity. Again, however, I stress that the purpose of this book is not to assess the morality of the affair. Arguments may be made on either side of that issue, and in any case, moral arguments usually do not have the power to sway lovers away from their chosen path. Having accepted the fact of the affair as given, however, does not excuse us from ethical responsibilities within the affair. And so the issue of your relative obligations to yourselves, to others, and to one another comes to the fore.

Where is the fairness in all this, you might ask, where is the justice? Why can you not "eat your cake and have it too," too? The mental contortions that are going to be required to analyze this possible third situation are going to require extreme moral flexibility and the capacity to twist your thinking into unfamiliar shapes. This is why I've affectionately and somewhat ironically nicknamed this third possibility "The Pretzel." Let's take its various elements one by one.

Sexual Aesthetics

For a long time, the word "aesthetics" was synonymous with "taste," as in "having good taste." The origin of the word in ancient Greek, "aesthesis," refers to *perception by the senses* – sight, hearing, taste, smell, touch

– particularly pertinent for our discussions about sex.

In today's times, it often seems old-fashioned to have hesitations about having more than one lover at a time. The truth of the matter is, however, that desires for sex and lovemaking are not the same sorts of desires and appetites as hunger for food or desire for a good therapeutic massage. This can create a problem for our third option.

Theoretically, a hunger for food can be satisfied by any number of things – soup, burgers, vegetables, ice cream, cheese, and so on. A desire for a good therapeutic massage can be taken care of by any number of licensed massage therapists, each of whom will have a different "touch" and each of whom will make you feel slightly different.

But when there is passionate love involved, we often find that the hunger or desire for sexual and emotional contact really can only be satisfied by *that one person* – that the desire is completely person-specific. At the same time, we may find (perhaps to our horror) that the thought of actually making love with anyone else, particularly during the time the love affair is active, fills us with revulsion or disgust. This is, of course, a serious problem when contemplating the possibility of developing a second, concurrent relationship with someone we could potentially consider a "mate." It is not likely that this person will be satisfied with a non-sexual relationship.

Of course, person-specific desire may be an irrelevant issue for you. In that case, you will find at least one of "The Pretzel's" problems easier to deal with.*

---

* I take as given an adult and informed concern with prevention of disease and pregnancy.

Ethics

This one is going to be more difficult. We noted earlier that every relationship carries certain obligations with it, and that usually these are relatively well-defined and obvious from the structure of the relationship and the names of the roles that people occupy in them. We further noted that this was not the case in an illicit love relationship such as an affair with a married person. This is where the issue of assessing your obligations becomes pressing. What, in fact, are your obligations in this third scenario, and how are you going to assess them?

We also spoke about the dynamics of a love affair – essentially, that it *feels* as though it is a normal or ordinary love relationship, even though it is very far from normal or ordinary and that moreover these powerful feelings are effectively more or less irrelevant to the day-to-day structure of lived life. This obviously has implications for the notion of fidelity within and outside the affair.

• Fidelity to Your Lover

In contemplating the option to carry on a dual lifestyle yourself, you might find that it feels as though you ought to be faithful to your lover and not engage in love relationships with other people while you are in the affair, because that is what your heart tells you. (We noted earlier that the heart is not sophisticated and only knows how to feel, not how to think.)

But as soon as you listen to your heart, your mind kicks in and reminds you of the 10% – 90% differential, and that your lover does not have to deal with this; your mind then asks you a very reasonable question: why should *you* have to deal with it? The endless dialogue with yourself that follows – once again, between your mind and your heart – will probably never be resolved. If you wish to maintain your affair, you can only decide to be "faithful" (but live alone, without a true mate), or to have another relationship (but be "unfaithful").

• Fidelity to a Potential New Lover

Furthermore, you and your lover are not the only ones to consider in making your decision. There is a person out there, somewhere, with whom you might feel comfortable enough to begin your second "90%" relationship; what are this person's rights? What obligations do you have to this person?

All the issues come up again and the internal dialogue takes on ever more sinister and mendacious tones. Fidelity: should you play it straight with this second person and leave your love affair? (*"Can't do that, don't want to do that, I never made any promises to this second person, I'm not "really" lying , . ."*) Secrecy: should you tell your lover you are beginning a second relationship? (*Either choice serves him or her right.*) Should you tell your second lover about your first lover? (*"Are you kidding? It's nobody's business who I spend my free time with. Caveat emptor!. . ."*)

Does this sound like the kind of rationalizing dialogue that you might have with yourself in such a circumstance? In that case, you ought to think about duplicity and lying, because that is what you are considering, regardless of the reasonable-sounding rationalizations. However, the question here is not whether these rationalizations are duplicitous; it is clear that they are. The question is whether there is a real justification for them. Is there? Perhaps. This is a genuine question and not just an evasion to avoid having to make a one-way-or-the-other choice. It is a nasty joke that life asks you to choose between love and fulfillment; it would be very easy to throw away ethics altogether.

To a great extent, the major ethical question concerns the possible second relationship that you would be getting into. It is one thing to be (for example) married, to realize gradually over the years that your marriage is not fulfilling or satisfying, that in spite of all your efforts in good faith, it cannot be repaired, and also to realize that it is impossible or undesirable to leave the marriage – if there are small children involved, or if you and your spouse are also business partners in a struggling enterprise, or if your spouse is handicapped in some way that would make it unethical and unkind for you to leave. At that point, the decision to live a dual life with someone else may be defensible – it is at least possible to see yourself as not having any real choices.

It is quite another thing to engage cold-bloodedly in a new relationship, without justifiable cause other than to satisfy your own self-interest, with your secret affair and its necessary lying a built-in part of the foundations of that new relationship. This is truly to use another human being as a means to an end, and in this case, it would be difficult to justify, no matter how genuine your feeling for this new person might be. This indeed is how some married persons actually do live their lives, in an active search for extramarital partners throughout the course of their marriages – infidelity as a chosen lifestyle (see the "Personals" section of almost any publication for verification of this).

On the other hand, it is tempting in your situation to

see yourself as the only person who is concerned about these sorts of ethical niceties, and to realize that your ethics may very well doom you to a life either lived alone or lived without passion. I have no answer for you, but I urge very careful consideration of the topics we have outlined above. The question of whether you have obligations to yourself of self-fulfillment is a serious one. It requires careful thought and weighing against the question of your current and potential obligations to others.

Integrity and Fragmentation

Unfortunately, the decision to engage in this sort of dual lifestyle is likely to get you back into a kind of pragmatic, necessary fragmentation and compartmentalization; you will have to build the same sort of rigid boundary between the two parts of your life as your married lover has. By the time the merely practical aspects of it are taken into account, for example, one lover calling while the other is there, you will find a great deal of your mental energy taken up with remembering what you said to whom and even what you did with whom. Which lover did you see that movie with? Which lover did you have that particular sexual experience with? Which lover has that special private joke with you? Your wholeness that you worked so hard to restore will now once again be split into two, and, significantly, your recognition of the Other (both Others) as a person is diminished, since you are using him or her merely to satisfy your own needs. The fact that it is you who are doing it to yourself and not your love affair that is doing it "to" you is beside the point. You are still fragmented again.

An amusing but ghastly recent television film highlights the extreme practical difficulties faced by a person who makes a decision to conduct secretly more than one serious relationship at a time. It depicted a physician who was married, simultaneously, to three women, all of whom were in approximately the same geographical region. He had to plan carefully a rotating schedule of being "home" for dinner and overnight with all three of them in sequence. He had to remember what he said to whom and what he promised to whom. He had to carry three mortgages and fill out three sets of tax returns. He had to carry a pager so no wife would call him at either of his other wives' homes. He had to deal with one wife dropping in at the hospital where he worked at the same time as another wife was doing volunteer work there, *and* at the same time, carry on a medical practice and take on more work so he could pay all the mortgages and other bills. He eventually died at an early age of a heart attack, at which point all the wives learned of one another's existence – an ugly legacy.

Certainly, this story is exaggerated for dramatic effect on television, but its kernels of both pragmatic and ethical truth bear thinking about.

The "State of the Union"

Of all these considerations the last and most important is what the mental, emotional, and spiritual state of your personhood will be after living a life underwritten by lying, deception, and secrecy. While it was your married lover living such a life, it was easy to see yourself on the periphery of moral obligation; after all, you could reason that you had little or nothing to do with the betrayed spouse – remember the assumption that there are likely to be no innocent adult victims in the eternal triangle – and you could easily tell yourself it was none of your business. (Again, to assess whether that is actually the case is not the purpose of these explorations.) Here, it is very much your business, since you are potentially the active, conscious betrayer of the trust of two people. Can you handle it? And why would you *want* to handle it – to get even with your married lover, to show your lover "what it feels like"? Very tempting, but again, inauthentic. To relieve your loneliness? Perhaps, but there may be worse things than being lonely.

A final consideration is that ethical questions such as these often conceal a double-edged sword. Honesty may very well be seen as a flight from responsibility in certain cases. For example, undergraduate philosophy students routinely assess the moral obligation of a straying wife to be to go home and tell her husband all about it. They support this course of action morally on the grounds of "honesty in the marriage" and have a great deal of difficulty wrapping their moral reasoning around the idea that honesty may not always be the best policy. Would not this straying wife be simply dumping her uncomfortable moral feelings upon her husband to relieve herself, but without much concern or sensitivity for his emotional well-being? She would possibly feel better after her confession, but he would be left with a package of knowledge that he did not ask for and perhaps did not want to know and will never be able to forget. In a case like this, it might very well be that silence would have been more moral than speaking about it.

Many people have to be taught this alternative viewpoint; it does not seem to occur to them naturally. Moreover, they often resist it on various grounds. A recent *Atlantic Monthly* exchange of letters concerned a similar example presented by Stephen L. Carter in his new book, *Integrity*. The letters took opposing views of whether a dying philanderer ought to inform his wife of his long-ago infidelity. Two of the three letters insisted upon the wife's being given full information on the grounds that she is *obligated*, as a human being, to "[do] the hard work of reconciling this fact about the marriage she was a party to with the fiction she had imagined." (Emphasis added.)[*]

The situation is only slightly different with "The Pretzel." Whether or not you also opt to take this omniscient and arrogant stance about what is good for others by virtue of their being human beings, bear in mind that your knowledge about your own life gives you the power to hurt seriously two people that you care for deeply; use your power wisely. If you happen to meet someone else while you are in the midst of your affair, and this new friendship grows into something serious while you are still in love with your married lover, the genuine question is whether your honesty would help or harm the two people you love. Perhaps at that point it would be responsible and moral for you to maintain silence until such time as you decide to leave one of these relationships. Even then, revealing the existence of either of these relationships to the other lover will probably cause hurt, confusion, and distrust. Deciding, on the other hand, to remain indefinitely in both relationships secretly will require an intestinal and moral fortitude that is very rare and perhaps harmful to you in the long run. It will also require the same strong sense of entitlement that we

[*] Stephen L. Carter, *Integrity* (New York, NY: Basic Books, 1996). *Atlantic Monthly*, "Letters," May, 1996.

spoke about earlier in relation to your married lover. Telling only one lover about the other is yet another possibility, but one that is likely to generate incredible tension and a terribly skewed dynamic, requiring a capacity for serious stress tolerance on your part. Arguably, it also dishonors the one who is kept in the dark. Again, I have no clear answer for you.

Here is a final exercise to try to find some way in addition to rational analysis of deciding some of these issues.

Exercise 12

The Inner Voice

This is a relaxation exercise which draws upon a particular understanding of our mental capacities. It is often said that we use only a small, conscious fraction of our minds to solve problems; this exercise will tap into a deep well of unconscious knowledge that you have about yourself and your situation, and will "pull" the beginnings of an answer for you out of this well. This is a technique used frequently by very creative people – scientists, artists, political leaders, and so on.

▪ Sitting quietly in a comfortable chair, relax; take several deep "cleansing" breaths and concentrate on relaxing your body. Beginning at your feet, consciously focus on relaxing all the muscles in your toes, the arch of your foot, and the top of your foot. Relax them completely – you will find that even though you might think they're relaxed enough already, by consciously focusing on them you will be releasing slight tensions that you were not aware of. When your feet are fully relaxed, move up to your ankles, your calves, thighs, stomach, chest, shoulders, arms, neck, and face. Do the same conscious, systematic relaxing at each part of your body, checking carefully for residual small tensions. Plan to spend enough time on this exercise for full relaxation in every area, working your way slowly up from your feet.

• You may find, when you are completely relaxed, that you feel some warmth in your fingertips and the palms of your hands, in your lower abdomen, or even in the soles of your feet. Some people feel warmth in their faces. These are normal reactions and indicate that your relaxation exercise is actually working and that you are, in fact, becoming more fully relaxed.

• When you feel you are fully relaxed, whether you feel any warmth or not, begin to think about your situation. Do not think "analytically" as we have been doing here in this series of explorations. Just let your mind wander aimlessly over images, thoughts, emotions, memories, and ideas about yourself and your life in this moment. Do not attempt to control the direction of your mind – just let it go. Your experience should be something like a long daydream, only you are fully conscious and relaxed. Do not edit or censor anything. If you come across something that disturbs you or makes you angry or anxious, just let your Observing Self take care of observing it and letting it pass, so you will not begin to tense up. If you begin to be distracted by irrelevant thoughts, push these ideas to one side with the intention of coming back to them later. It is important that you stay focused on your particular dilemma in the moment. Let yourself have this daydream in a perfectly relaxed state for as long as you like – 15 minutes is usually enough, but go ahead for longer if you like.

▪ When you are ready to end this exercise and get on with your day, you come to the most important part of this exercise: give yourself an "assignment" to make a decision by a certain time, for example, "by next Monday." Then, go on about your business and don't think about it any more. You will find, if you have done this exercise conscientiously in the relaxing stage, and for long enough in the daydreaming stage, that it is likely that your unconscious mind will have an answer for you by the deadline you have set. "Tomorrow morning" or "next Monday" you will wake up and have an idea what you will do. If you do not have a clear enough answer, do the exercise again.

Comments:

As I have said, this is a reliable technique used by many creative people. When the dilemma or problem they are working on seems insoluble, they recognize that there is probably information that is necessary for the resolution of the problem buried somewhere in their unconscious. Often this technique works even when they do not consciously choose to use it. They typically break their heads over the problem, then after a long period of time without any progress, they give up in disgust and go do something else. Within several days, they will have an unexpected "Eureka!" experience or some flash of insight that leads to a resolution, because they have been working nonstop "underground" on the problem while they were mentally busy elsewhere.

People have long recognized this human intellectual

capacity and have figured out how to elicit this experience deliberately. The exercise I have given you is one
way to do so.

Conclusion: Freedom

We have now come to the end of this series of discussions on surviving a love affair. We have explored carefully the various aspects of such love relationships – their intensity, beauty, and grace, as well as the destruction and suffering they usually foster. Through a series of precisely targeted exercises, you have had the opportunity to learn a great deal about yourself. Some of this will have brought new and maybe surprising knowledge, and some may have been already familiar to you but largely forgotten because of the intense emotional and mental demands of your love affair. Finally, you have looked at how it might be possible to put all this knowledge about yourself and your relationship to work in order to make the difficult choices necessary to make yourself whole and to change your life. You have examined the possibilities both of leaving and of staying, and you have considered both the desirable and undesirable outcomes of these choices.

What is the next step for you after you have finished exploring these issues through this book? Here I am going to depart from what might be expected, and remind you that there is no one watching your clock. These have not been traditional goal-setting self-help exercises; there is no timetable and no required next step, because part of being free is recognizing your freedom to do something, to do nothing, or to sleep on it indefinitely. The essential factor is choosing an option consciously and with full awareness. The purpose of these meditations and exercises, then, was not to get you to *do* something according to some implicit agenda; the purpose was rather to get you to *be* something: a free person.

Perhaps you will think this is presumptuous – who am I, after all, to try to get you to be something of my own choosing? After all, is that not following an agenda of some sort? And how do I know that being free is the right thing for you to be?

I will let Aristotle, a 4th-century B.C. philosopher and arguably the greatest of all time, answer that question for me. In his *Nichomachean Ethics* he offers us a complete analysis of the systematic connections between human reason, desire, intention, and action, and what end or goal all these ought to work toward in a fully-functional or self-actualized person.

Briefly, he proposed part of that end or goal as human excellence, or "virtue." He defined virtue as a state of character concerned with choice, and defined the purpose of choice as taking action following deliberation. Further, he asserted that one can only be seen to be virtuous when one's passions and actions are voluntary and fully conscious. Compare Aristotle's "virtuous action" with our early discussion of "effective action."

It appears that the essential combination *deliberation-choice-action* is not available except to those who are free, who act *voluntarily*. Aristotle underlines this point by stressing that we cannot be either praised or blamed for our *involuntary* actions, but he insists on extremely strict criteria for naming an action involuntary. He says we may be excused from responsibility for our actions either if we are ignorant of the particular circumstances of a situation or if we are externally compelled to perform an act and we, as agents, contribute nothing at all to the action. However, we can never be excused for our ignorance of the general principles of right action. It appears clear that freedom is necessary in order to deliberate, to make voluntary choices, and to act.

What about the ends or goals of the self-actualized human person? Aristotle tells us we aim for happiness, and after some consideration of what happiness is (and isn't), he arrives at an understanding of what is really good for us, what will truly make us happy: the activity of soul which either understands rational principles or is prepared to obey such principles; in other words, "...the activity of the soul in accordance with virtue" (or excellence). This activity of the soul leads us to true happiness, a self-sufficient good – "...that which...makes life desirable and lacking in nothing."

It is clear that the pursuit of happiness, a self-sufficient good and an end in itself, requires some knowledge or understanding of what constitutes virtue, but this knowledge cannot be obtained if we continue to allow ourselves to be imprisoned by our passions and obsessions. Reflect on our previous discussions of passivity and helplessness, the flight from freedom, and imprisonment by illusion, emotion, and obsessive thinking. The key common element in all these is the inability or refusal to recognize our own freedom to choose, to think clearly, to feel authentically, and to act effectively.

This has been my purpose in structuring these discussions, exercises, and meditations – to foster your own growth as a free person, to nurture the freedom that can help you break out of the various kinds of bondage that love affairs tend to impose. And note my certainly controversial assumption, in disagreement with Aristotle, that persons in love affairs can also be considered to share in human virtue, provided that their decisions are made voluntarily, with awareness and sensitivity to the human condition that they share with their lovers and their lovers' spouses.

I hope you have found this series of explorations helpful and that my actions in compiling them have been effective for you. They will have been effective if what you end up doing is something that you now freely choose to do.